At War with Pontiac
The Totem of the Bear

Kirk Munroe and J. Finnemore

Contents

CHAPTER I TAWTRY HOUSE 7
CHAPTER II THE MAJOR GAINS A FRIEND AND MAKES AN ENEMY 11
CHAPTER III TRUMAN FLAGG'S STORY 15
CHAPTER IV ESCAPE OF THE PRISONERS 18
CHAPTER V A BABY LOST AND RECOVERED 22
CHAPTER VI THE WILDERNESS 26
CHAPTER VII THE MAJOR RE-ENTERS ACTIVE SERVICE 29
CHAPTER VIII DONALD SETS FORTH ON A PERILOUS MISSION 33
CHAPTER IX ST. AUBIN'S STARTLING INFORMATION 37
CHAPTER X PONTIAC DECLARES WAR 41
CHAPTER XI MAJOR HESTER IS TAKEN PRISONER 45
CHAPTER XII DONALD AT JOHNSON CASTLE 49
CHAPTER XIII PAYMASTER BULLEN AND HIS WONDERFUL TUB 54
CHAPTER XIV A WHITE MEDICINE MAN 58
CHAPTER XV DONALD AND CHRISTIE CEMENT A FRIENDSHIP 62
CHAPTER XVI QUICKEYE AND THE "ZEBRA" 67
CHAPTER XVII A BRAVE GIRL CAPTIVE 72
CHAPTER XVIII SURPRISE AND DESTRUCTION OF THE BOAT BRIGADE 76
CHAPTER XIX THE TOTEM SAVES DONALD'S LIFE 81
CHAPTER XX BITTER DISAPPOINTMENT AT FORT DETROIT 85
CHAPTER XXI IN SEARCH OF A LOST SISTER 90
CHAPTER XXII AMID THE RUINS OF FORT SANDUSKY 94
CHAPTER XXIII DISCOVERED AND PURSUED BY SAVAGES 98
CHAPTER XXIV CHRISTIE'S BRAVE DEFENCE OF HIS POST 103
CHAPTER XXV DONALD FIRES THE MINE AND SAVES THE BLOCKHOUSE 107
CHAPTER XXVI FRIENDS IN CAPTIVITY 112
CHAPTER XXVII HOW THE PAYMASTER NAVIGATED LAKE ERIE IN A TUB 117
CHAPTER XXVIII THE PAYMASTER IN WAR-PAINT AND FEATHERS 122
CHAPTER XXIX DONALD AND THE PAYMASTER ESCAPE 127
CHAPTER XXX IMMINENT DANGER OF THE SCHOONER GLADWYN 131
CHAPTER XXXI PONTIAC RECOGNIZES THE TOTEM 136
CHAPTER XXXII LAST CRUISE OF THE PAYMASTER'S TUB 141
CHAPTER XXXIII FORT DETROIT IS REINFORCED 146
CHAPTER XXXIV AH-MO, THE DAUGHTER OF PONTIAC 150
CHAPTER XXXV A NIGHT OF FIGHTING AND TERROR 154
CHAPTER XXXVI BRAVE DEATH OF THE OLD MAJOR 159
CHAPTER XXXVII THE CURSE OF THE MAGIC CIRCLE 163
CHAPTER XXXVIII A WINTER IN THE WILDERNESS 168
CHAPTER XXXIX AN ADOPTED DAUGHTER OF THE FOREST 173
CHAPTER XL THE PRINCESS ANSWERS DONALD'S QUESTION 178

AT WAR WITH PONTIAC
THE TOTEM OF THE BEAR

BY

Kirk Munroe and J. Finnemore

AT WAR WITH PONTIAC
OR THE TOTEM OF THE BEAR

CHAPTER I
TAWTRY HOUSE

A glorious midsummer day was drawing to a close; its heat had passed; the tall forest trees, whose leaves were pleasantly rustled by the cool breeze of approaching night, flung a bridge of tremulous shadows across the surface of Loch Meg, and all nature was at peace. The tiny lake, though bearing an old-world name, was of the new world, and was one of the myriad forest gems that decked the wilderness of western New York a century and a half ago. It was embraced in a patent recently granted by the English king to his well-approved servant Graham Hester, whose bravery and wounds had won for him an honorable retirement, with the rank of major in a Highland regiment, ere he was forty years of age. Being thus provided with an ample estate, Major Hester, with his young wife and half a dozen trusty followers, left the old world for the new, and plunged into its wilderness. Though somewhat dismayed to find his property located a score of leagues beyond that of his nearest white neighbor, the major was at the same time gratified to discover in that neighbor his old friend and comrade, William Johnson, through whose diplomacy the powerful Iroquois tribes of the Six Nations were allied to the English and kept at peace.

On a crest of land overlooking and sloping gently down to the blue lakelet which Major Hester had named in honor of his wife, he erected a substantial block-house of squared timbers. Behind it were ranged a number of log outbuildings about three sides of a square, in the centre of which was dug a deep well. Having thus in a time of peace prepared for war, the proprietor began the improvement of his estate with such success that, within three years from the felling of the first tree, several acres of gloomy forest were replaced by smiling fields. A young orchard was in sturdy growth, a small herd of cattle found ample pasturage on the borders of the lake, and on all sides were evidences of thrift and plenty.

The military instinct of the proprietor caused all forest growth to be cleared from a broad space entirely around the rude fortress that held his life's treasures; but within the enclosure he left standing two superb oaks. These not only afforded a grateful shade, but gave a distinctive feature to the place that was quickly recognized by the surrounding Indians. Thus they always spoke of it as the house of the two trees, or two-tree house, a name that soon became "Tawtry House," under which designation it was known from the unsalted seas to the tide waters of the distant Shattemuc.

Tawtry House not only offered a ready welcome and bountiful hospitality to the occasional hunter, trader, or traveller tempted by business or curiosity into that wild region, but to the Indians who still roamed the forest at will and had established one of their villages at no great distance from it. With these, by the exercise of extreme firmness and an inflexible honesty, Major Hester succeeded in maintaining friendly relations, in spite of their jealousy of his presence among them. At the same time, his wife, through her gentleness and ready sympathy in their times of sickness or distress, gained their deep-seated affection.

Although the Iroquois were thus at peace with their English neighbors, there was a bitter enmity between them and the French settlers of Canada, who had espoused the cause of their hereditary foes, the tribes dwelling along the St. Lawrence and on both shores of the great fresh-water lakes. Most prominent of these were the Ottawas, Hurons or Wyandots, Ojibwas and Pottawattamies, who were allied in a defensive league against their powerful enemies. Their ancient hatred of the Iroquois, animated by the traditions of generations, was ever fanned into a blaze by Jesuit priests eager for the triumph of their faith, French traders anxious to monopolize the immensely profitable fur business of the new world, and French soldiers determined at any cost to extend the empire of their king. Thus, on one pretext or another, war parties were constantly coming and going, destroying or being destroyed, and it well behooved the adventurous frontier settler to intrench himself strongly behind massive timbers and stout palisades.

Under these conditions and amid such scenes, in the year 1743, when Tawtry House was still sweet-scented with odors of the forest from which it had been so recently hewn, was born Donald Hester, as sturdy a young American as ever kicked in swaddling clothes, and the hero of this tale of the forest.

On the midsummer evening with which our story opens, Major Hester and his wife walked, hand in hand, beyond the palisades of their fortress home, enjoying the marvellous beauty of their surroundings and talking of many things. Already had this wilderness home become very dear to them; for, representing years of toil and privation as it did, it was their very own and the heritage of their boy, now two years of age, who toddled behind them in charge of a ruddy-cheeked Scotch nurse. While they rejoiced over what had been accomplished, they planned for the future, and discussed the details of many projected improvements. At the outlet of the lake a grist-mill should be built, and the low lands beyond should be drained to afford increased pasturage for their multiplying herd.

As they talked there came a sound from the forest depths that caused them to pause and listen. Borne faintly on the evening breeze, was a distant firing of guns, and they fancied that it was accompanied by a confusion of yells from human throats.

"Oh, Graham! what can it mean?" exclaimed Mrs. Hester, as she clasped her husband's arm and glanced instinctively back, to make sure of the safety of her child.

"Nothing that need alarm you, my dear," answered the major, reassuringly. "It is only a token of some jollification among our Indian friends: a war dance, or a scalp dance, or the advent among them of a new lot of wretched captives, or something of that kind. I remember Truman mentioning, more than a week ago, that another war party had gone out. I do wish though that the Senecas would take it into their heads to move their village farther away. I used to think five miles quite a respectable distance, but now--"

"I would that this horrible fighting were ended," interrupted Mrs. Hester. "Will not the time ever come, Graham, when these poor heathen will cease from their dreadful wars, and live at peace with each other, like civilized beings?"

"Like civilized beings, my dear?" laughed Major Hester. "Yes, I think I may safely prophesy that if the time ever comes when those nations which we call civilized give over fighting, then even the red Indians may be persuaded to follow their example. As for their methods of warfare, they are but the counterparts of those practised by our own savage ancestors a few centuries ago; while in their torture of captives they are only reproducing the acts of civilized Romans, mediaeval knights, and the Holy Inquisition. It is not long since, even in England, Elizabeth Gaunt was burned to death at Tyburn for yielding to the dictates of compassion and giving shelter to a political offender; nor are the cries for mercy of the martyrs tortured at Smithfield stakes yet forgotten. The torture of New England witches is recent history, while the dismal record of devilish tortures inflicted by white men upon Indian captives is unbroken from the days of Columbus. Did not Frontenac cause an Iroquois warrior to be burned alive in order to terrorize his fellows? Did not--"

The honest major was so warmed to his subject that he might have discoursed upon it indefinitely, had he not been startlingly interrupted. He and his wife were retracing their steps toward the house, and, as before, the Scotch maid, with her toddling charge, was some paces behind them. At a wild scream from the girl those in advance turned in time to see the flying form of a young Indian, who had just emerged from the near-by forest, fall headlong at her feet. His naked body was pierced by wounds, and his strength was evidently exhausted. As he fell, a second Indian, in whose right hand gleamed a deadly tomahawk, leaped from the woodland shadows, and, with a yell of triumph, bounded toward his intended victim. He was closely followed by two others.

As the Scotch girl stood motionless with terror, little Donald, evidently believing this to be some new form of game provided for his especial edification, ran forward with a gurgle of delight, stumbled, and fell directly across the head of the prostrate Indian. But for the child's sudden movement the keen-bladed hatchet in the hand of the foremost pursuer, already drawn back for the deadly throw, would have sped on its fatal mission.

With a cry of anguish Mrs. Hester sprang toward her baby; but quicker than she, with a leap like that of a panther, Major Hester gained the spot first, snatched up his child, and, over the body of the young Indian, sternly confronted his scowling pursuers.

CHAPTER II
THE MAJOR GAINS A FRIEND
AND MAKES AN ENEMY

For some seconds the three Indians, who were panting heavily from the effect of their long chase through the forest, gazed in silence at the white man who with the child in his arms so fearlessly confronted them. Then the foremost of them, an evil-looking savage who bore the name of Mahng (the Diver), motioned the major aside with a haughty wave of the hand, saying: "Let the white man step from the path of Mahng, that he may kill this Ottawa dog who thought to escape the vengeance of the Senecas."

Without retreating an inch from his position, and still holding the little Donald, who crowed with delight at sight of the Indians, Major Hester replied:--

"Not even if the whole Seneca tribe demanded it would I allow this man to be murdered in the presence of my wife. Nor, since my child has saved his life, will I deliver him into your hands for torture. He has sought my protection, and it shall be granted him until he is proved unworthy of it. Let the sachems of your tribe lay this grievance before Sir William Johnson. If the white chief decides that the prisoner must be restored to them, and so orders, then will I give him up, but not before. Now go, ere my young men, who are already approaching, reach this place and drive you from it with whips, like yelping curs."

Being sufficiently acquainted with the English language to comprehend the purport of these remarks, the scowling savage made answer:--

"Who gave the white man the right to step between an Indian and an Indian? This land is Indian land. The long house in which the white man dwells belongs to the Indians, as did the forest trees from which it is built. If the Indian says stay, then may you stay; if he says go, then must you go. Let one of your young men but lift a hand against Mahng, and this ground that has known the tread of the white man shall know it no more forever. His house shall become a hooting place for owls, and Seneca squaws shall gather the harvest of his fields. Restore then to Mahng his prisoner, that there may be no bad blood between him and his white brother."

"Never," replied Major Hester, who was sufficiently versed in the Indian tongue to catch the general drift of these remarks.

He had hardly uttered the word ere Mahng stooped, darted forward with deadly intent like a wild serpent, and sought to bury his gleaming hatchet in the brain of his still prostrate foe.

Like a flash the major's strong right foot shot out; the heavy, hob-nailed walking-shoe caught the savage squarely under the chin; he was lifted from the ground, and, falling on his back, lay as one who is dead.

The remaining savages made as though to take instant vengeance for this deadly insult and, as they imagined, murder of their leader, but their impulse was checked by a stern command from behind. Glancing in that direction, they saw themselves covered by a long, brown rifle-barrel, held by a white man clad in the leathern costume of the backwoods. At the same time half a dozen laborers who, home-returning from the fields, had noticed that something unusual was taking place, came hurrying to the scene of disturbance. Wisely concluding that under these circumstances discretion was the better part of valor, the Senecas picked up their helpless comrade and, retreating as rapidly as their burden would permit, disappeared amid the darkening shadows of the forest.

The tableau presented at this moment by those who remained was that of the tall major standing above the prostrate form of the escaped captive, holding his laughing child in one arm while his trembling wife clung to the other. Close beside them knelt the terror-stricken maid, with her face buried in her hands, and a few paces in the rear were grouped the laborers, armed with various implements of toil. In the foreground, Truman Flagg, the hunter, white by birth, Indian by association and education, leaned on his rifle and gazed silently after the disappearing savages. As they vanished in the forest, he remarked quietly:--

"'Twas handsomely done, major, and that scoundrel Mahng deserved all he got. But ef he's as dead as he looks, I'm fearful that kick may get you into trouble with the tribe, though he's not a Seneca by blood, nor overly popular at that."

"You know him, then?" queried the major.

"Not edzackly what you might call know him; but I know something of him."

"Very well; come up to the house and tell me what you know, while we consider this business. Some of you men carry this poor fellow to the tool-house, where we will see what can be done for him. Now, my dear, the evening meal awaits us, and I for one shall partake of it with a keener relish that this unfortunate affair has terminated so happily."

"I pray God, Graham, that it may be terminated," replied Mrs. Hester, fervently, as she took the child from its father's arms and strained him to her bosom.

The whole of this dramatic scene had transpired within the space of a few minutes, and when the men approached to lift the prostrate Indian they found him so recovered from his exhaustion as to be able to stand, and walk feebly with the aid of some support.

Major Hester's first duty, after conveying his wife and child to the shelter of the blockhouse, was to visit the guest so strangely thrust upon his hospitality and inquire into his condition. He found him lying on a pallet of straw, over which a blanket had been thrown, and conversing with Truman Flagg in an Indian tongue unknown to the proprietor. The hunter was bathing the stranger's wounds with a gentleness that seemed out of keeping with his own rude aspect, and administering occasional draughts of cool well water, that appeared to revive the sufferer as though it were the very elixir of life.

"What do you make of the case?" asked the major, as he watched Truman Flagg apply to each of the many gashes in the Indian's body a healing salve made of bear's grease mixed with the fragrant resin of the balsam fir. "Will he pull through, think you?"

"Bless you, yes, major! He'll pull through all right; for, bad as his hurts look, none of em's dangerous. They warn't meant to be. He was nighest dead from thirst. You see, he's been under torture most of the day, without nary a drop to wash down his last meal, which war a chunk of salted meat give to him yesterday evening. He'll pick up fast enough now, though. All he needs to make him as good as new is food and drink, and a night's rest. After that you'll find him ready to go on the war-path again, ef so be he's called to do it. He's the pluckiest Injun ever I see, and I've trailed, fust and last, most of the kinds there is. Ef he warn't, I wouldn't be fussin' over him now, for his tribe is mostly pizen. But true grit's true grit, whether you find it in white or red, and a man what values hisself as a man, is bound to appreciate it whenever its trail crosses his'n."

"A sentiment in which I must heartily concur," assented the major. "A brave enemy is always preferable to a cowardly friend. But is this Indian an enemy? To what tribe does he belong?"

"Ottaway," was the laconic answer.

"Ottawa!" exclaimed the major, greatly disconcerted. "Why, the Ottawas are the firmest allies of France and the most inveterate enemies of the English. Are you certain he is an Ottawa?"

"Sartain," replied the hunter, with a silent laugh at the other's evident dismay. "And not only that, but he's the best fighter and best man in the whole Ottaway tribe. They call him Songa, the strong heart, and I consate Sir William would be passing glad to exchange one hundred pounds of the king's money for his scalp to-morrow."

"Why don't you earn it, then?" asked, the other. "Surely one hundred pounds could not be gained more easily, nor is it a sum of money to be despised even by an independent American woods-ranger like yourself."

For answer the hunter rose slowly to his full height, and, holding a candle above his head, so that its light shone full on the proprietor's face, regarded him intently for a score of seconds.

"You don't mean it, Major Hester! Thank God, you don't mean it! for your face belies your words, and proves you to be an honest man," he said at length. "Ef I thought you meant what you just said, and was one to tempt a poor man to commit a murder for the sake of gold, I would never again sit at your table, nor set foot in your house, nor look upon your face, nor think of you save with the contempt an honest man must always feel for a villain."

"No, Truman. I did not mean what I said," replied the major, holding out a hand that was heartily grasped by the other. "I spoke out of curiosity to hear your reply, though I might have known it would have the ring of true steel. Now I must return to my wife, and if you will join us, after you have done what you can for this poor fellow, we will consult concerning the situation, for it is no light thing to hold Songa the Ottawa as prisoner in one's house."

CHAPTER III
TRUMAN FLAGG'S STORY

Truman Flagg was a son of one of those hardy New England families which, ever pushing into the wilderness in the extreme van of civilization, were the greatest sufferers from the forays of French and Indians, who every now and then swept down from Canada, like packs of fierce Northern wolves. In one of these raids his parents were killed, and the lad was borne away to be adopted among the Caughnawagas, who dwelt on the St. Lawrence, not far from Montreal. With these Indians he lived for several years, and having a natural taste for languages, acquired, during this time, a fair knowledge of the tongues of most of the Northern tribes, as well as a smattering of French. He also became well versed in woodcraft, and so thoroughly Indian in appearance and habit that when he was again captured by a marauding party of Maquas, or Mohawks, it was not detected that he was of white blood until he was stripped for the ordeal of the gantlet, in an Iroquois village. His identity being thus discovered, his latest captors washed from him his Caughnawaga paint, repainted and reclad him in Mohawk fashion, and treated him in all respects like a son of the tribe. Having thus exchanged one form of Indian life for another, Truman Flagg remained among the Iroquois long enough to master their languages, and receive the name of Honosagetha, or the man of much talk. Finally, he attracted the attention of Sir William Johnson, and became one of the general's interpreters, as well as a counsellor in Indian affairs. After awhile the forest ranger so fretted against the restraints of civilization and town life, as he termed that of the frontier settlement clustered about Johnson Hall on the lower Mohawk, that when Major Hester, searching for an experienced guide and hunter, offered him the position, he gladly accepted it. Since then, save when his services were required as a messenger between Tawtry House and the river settlements, he had been free to come and go as he pleased, provided he kept his employer fairly well provided with all varieties of game in its season. Thus he was able to spend much of his time in roaming the forest, passing from one Indian village to another, keeping himself posted on all subjects of interest to these wilderness communities, and ever watching, with eagle eye, over the safety of the Tawtry House inmates. He was a simple-hearted fellow, of sterling honesty, and a keen intelligence, that enabled him to absorb information on all subjects that came within his range, as a sponge absorbs water. Although of slender build, his muscles were of iron, his eyesight was that of a hawk, and as a rifle-shot he had no superior among all the denizens of the forest, white or red. During three years of mutual helpfulness, a strong friendship had sprung up between this son of the forest and the soldier, whose skilled valor on old-world battle-fields had won the approbation of a king. Now, therefore, the latter awaited with impatience the coming of the hunter, whose advice he deemed essential before deciding upon any plan of action in the present crisis.

When Truman Flagg appeared, and reported his patient to be sleeping soundly after having eaten a hearty supper, the major asked what he knew concerning the young Ottawa, and was answered as follows:--

"As fur as I kin make out, major, Mahng, the fellow you laid out so neatly awhile ago, is a Jibway, while Songa is an Ottaway, and son of the head chief, or medicine man, of the Metai, a magic circle of great influence among the lake tribes. Not long ago both Songa and Mahng courted a young Jibway squaw, who was said to be the handsomest gal of her tribe. They had some hot fights over her; but from the first she favored Songa, and so, of course, the other fellow had no show. Finally, Songa married her and carried her away to the Ottaway villages. On this, Mahng swore to be revenged on both of 'em, and as the Jibways and Ottaways is good friends, he come and jined the Senecas on purpose to get a chance at Songa. Here, seeing as he belongs to the totem of the wolf, which is strong among the Senecas, and as he isn't in noways a coward nor lacking in good fighting sense, he soon made a name for himself as a warrior, and could raise a party agin the Ottaways any time he chose. Most of the fighting that's been going on since you came here has been stirred up by Mahng, and ef the whites gets drawed into it, it'll be his doings. With all his smartness he never met up with Songa, or leastways never got the best of him, till this last time, when, fur as I kin make out, they caught him and his squaw and their young one travelling from one Ottaway village to another. They say Songa made the prettiest fight ever was seen, killed half a dozen of Mahnga party, and held 'em all off till his squaw had made good her escape with the child. Then he give up, and they brought him in. They waited till he got well of his hurts, and then they set out to kill him by as mean and devilish a lot of tortures as ever I see."

"You don't mean to say," interrupted the other, "that you were one of the spectators at a scene of torture, and did nothing to prevent it?"

"Sartain I do, major. It's part of my business to see such things. It's also part of my business to keep the peace, so fur as I kin, betwixt Injuns and whites, which it would have been broke very sudden ef I had interfered with an Injun execution of an Injun captive. They was only acting 'cording to their light, and I acted 'cording to mine."

"I suppose you are right," assented the major, "but I am glad I was not in your place, and sorry that the savages should have had the encouragement of your presence at one of their devilish orgies."

"They've had that many a time, major, when I couldn't help myself," replied the hunter, soberly. "They didn't get any encouraging from me this day, though, for they didn't see me. I was too snugly hid for that. But to make a short story, they tormented that poor chap in one way and another until I thought he must be done for, and all the time he never uttered a sound except to jeer at 'em, nor quivered an eyelash. Once, when they saw he was nearly dead with thirst, they loosed his hands and gave him a bowl of cool spring water; but as he lifted it to his lips, they dashed it to the ground. After that they held another bowl of water close to his face, but he never gratified 'em by making a move to try and drink it.

"Finally, they made a circle of dry wood around him and set fire to it. Then I thought it was all up with the poor fellow, and his torment would soon be over. I was just saying this to myself when something swift and still as a shadder brushed past the place where I was hid. I had just time to see that it was a woman, when she cleared the woods like a flash, ran to the stake, never minding the flames more'n ef they'd been a shower of rain, and cut Songa free.

"He gave a great leap, like a deer, out of the ring of fire that was slowly roasting him, knocked down two or three warriors that stood in his path, and gained the woods, with her close beside him, almost before any one knew what had happened. A score of rifle balls whizzed after them, but they wasn't hit, and they had a clear start of a hundred yards afore the crowd took after 'em. Mahng was the only one who could keep 'em in sight, and when they separated at the foot of the lake, he taking up one side, and she the other, Mahng trailed the one he hated most, which was Songa."

"How did you happen to see all this?" inquired the major. "They must have passed from view of your hiding-place very quickly."

"Oh, I jined in the hunt, too," replied Truman Flagg. "I thought some one might find it handy to have me 'round. Besides, I was feeling cramped and in need of a bit of exercise."

"Well, it was handy to have you around," said the major, heartily, "and it will be long ere I forget the gratitude with which I saw you at that critical moment. I am thankful, too, that the poor fellow escaped and sought the refuge he did, though what I am to do with him is more than I can imagine. I wish with all my heart that he were well on his way toward the Ottawa villages. But who was the woman who rescued him so splendidly, and what do you suppose became of her?"

"He claims her as his squaw," replied the hunter, "and ef she's where I left her, she's setting watching him at this moment."

"You don't mean it! How can she be?" cried the major, jumping to his feet.

"I do mean it; and she can be beside him because I let her in myself, not half an hour ago, and locked the door after me when I come out."

"Then come with me at once, for I must go and see them," exclaimed the proprietor, starting toward the door.

"Hold a bit, major. Don' you think that maybe Songa has earned a few hours of uninterrupted rest?" asked the hunter.

"Yes, you are right, he certainly has," replied the major, as he again sank into his chair.

CHAPTER IV
ESCAPE OF THE PRISONERS

Mrs. Hester, who had been putting her child to sleep, entered the room in time to hear the conclusion of the hunter's story, which she found intensely interesting. Like her husband, she was filled with a desire to see the brave woman who, daring all for the man she loved, had, alone and unaided, saved him from a horrible fate.

With him, though, she agreed that it would be cruel to disturb the much-needed and bravely earned rest of their guests. Thus it was decided that they should wait until morning before visiting those whom Fate had so strangely thrust upon their hospitality. In the meantime, were they guests or prisoners, and what was to be done with them? Long and animated was the discussion of these questions, which were finally settled by the major, who said: "They are both. For this night they are our guests. To-morrow morning I shall set a guard over them, for their protection as well as our own. Thus they will become prisoners. If by the time the Ottawa warrior is sufficiently recovered of his wounds to travel, I have received no word to the contrary from Johnson, I shall let him go, and bid him God speed. If, however, I should receive orders to continue to hold him, or even to deliver him over to his savage captors, which God forbid, I can conceive of no alternative save that of obedience."

"Oh, Graham! You wouldn't, you couldn't, deliver that splendid Indian and his brave wife to the awful fate that would await them!" cried Mrs. Hester.

"I don't think that I could give up the woman nor that I would be required to, seeing that she was not a prisoner of war; but with the man it is different. He is a chief in the tribe who have proved themselves most inveterate foes of the English, and, from what Flagg tells me, I should judge a man of extraordinary ability. His death at this time might prove the future salvation of hundreds of white men, women, and children. To allow him to escape may involve us in war. The decision either way will be fraught with far-reaching results, and I am thankful that it does not rest with me. Whatever Johnson may order in a case of this kind must be obeyed, without regard to our private views, for he is the accredited representative, in this section, of the king, God bless him, whom we are sworn to serve. At any rate, we may rest easy this night, and for two yet to come; for, even if the Senecas lay this grievance before the governor, it must still be several days ere I can hear from him."

"Oh dear!" sighed Mrs. Hester, "I suppose you are right, Graham, of course, but the contingency is too dreadful to contemplate. I believe I would even go so far as to help these poor people to escape, and so defy the governor, rather than allow them to be given up; for I know the wife will insist on sharing her husband's fate, whatever it may be."

"I don't believe you would, my dear, if you first paused to consider what effect your action might have upon the future of your own boy," replied her husband, gravely.

Before retiring for the night the major and Truman Flagg cautiously approached the tool-house, and, listening at its single open window, which was merely a slit cut through the logs at the back to serve as a loop-hole for musketry, plainly heard the heavy breathing that assured them of the safety of the prisoners. Then the major bade his companion good-night, and turned toward his own quarters. He had gone but a few steps when the hunter overtook him and handed him the key of the tool-house, saying that he should feel more at ease with it in the proprietor's possession. As they again separated, he remarked that being so very weary, he feared he should sleep late the following morning.

In spite of this, Truman Flagg was up and stirring while it yet wanted an hour of dawn. Lighting a small dark-lantern and moving with the utmost caution, he made, from various places, a collection of food, clothing, and arms.

"It's what the major in his heart wishes done, I'm sartain," he muttered to himself, "and what the madam would never forgive me ef I left undone. I could see that in her face."

Having completed his preparations, the hunter stepped lightly across the parade ground, as the major called the enclosed square, and opened the tool-house door, which he had softly unlocked, in anticipation of this time, the moment before handing its key to Major Hester. Carefully as he entered the building, its inmates were instantly wide awake and aware of his presence. With a few whispered words he explained the situation to Songa, adding that while the white chief had no authority to free a prisoner, he was unwilling that one whose life had been saved by his child should be restored to those who would surely kill him. "Therefore," continued the hunter, "he bids you make good your escape while it is yet dark, taking with you these presents. He would have you tell no man of the manner of your going, and bids you remember, if ever English captives are in your power, that you owe both life and liberty to an English child."

"To you," he added, turning to Songa's heroic wife, "the white squaw sends the greeting of one brave woman to another. She bids you go in peace, lead your husband to the lodges of his people, and restore him to the child who, but for her child, would now be fatherless."

As the young Ottawa, assisted by his loving wife, slowly gained his feet and painfully straightened his body, whose stiffened wounds rendered every movement one of torture, he answered simply:--

"The words of my white brother are good. Songa will never forget them. If all white men were like him, there would be no more fighting, for the hatchet would be buried forever."

While both the hunter and the squaw rubbed the sufferer's limbs with bear's grease, and so in a measure restored their suppleness, the latter said in a low voice, that was yet thrilling in its intensity:--

"Tell my white sister that through her words I can understand the love of the Great Spirit for his children. They have sunk deep into my heart, where their refreshing shall ever be as that of cool waters."

In the first faint flush of the coming dawn two dusky figures slipped, with the silence of shadows, from among the buildings of Tawtry House, sped across the open, and vanished in the blackness of the forest. At the same time Truman Flagg, well satisfied with the act just performed, though wondering as to what would be its results, returned to his own lodging, flung himself on his couch of skins, and was quickly buried in slumber.

He was awakened some time later by the voice of his employer, calling, "Come, Flagg! Turn out! the sun is all of two hours high, and here you are still sleeping. You ought to be ashamed of yourself."

As the hunter emerged from his cabin, yawning and stretching, the major continued: "I am on my way to visit our guests, or prisoners, as I suppose we must now call them, and want you to act as interpreter. Whether guests or prisoners, we must not allow them to starve, and if they are half as hungry as I am at this moment, they must feel that they are in imminent danger of it."

The honest soldier was amazed to find the door of the tool-house unlocked, and still more so to discover that the place was empty. "What does it mean?" he cried angrily. "Have we a traitor among us? or is it witchcraft? Surely no human being, wounded so nigh unto death as was that Indian but a few hours since, could have effected an escape unaided."

"You forget that the squaw was with him," suggested the hunter.

"True; though how she could have unlocked the door passes my understanding. Are you certain that you locked it after admitting her?"

"I am sartain," replied Truman Flagg, "for I tried it afterwards."

A prolonged, though unavailing, search was made through all the buildings and the adjacent forest that morning. While it was in progress the major appeared greatly chagrined at the turn of events; but his outward demeanor concealed an inward satisfaction that he had not been obliged to abuse the laws of hospitality, by treating his guests as prisoners.

As for Mrs. Hester, she rejoiced so openly at their escape that the hunter was finally emboldened to confess to her his share in it, and deliver the message of the Indian woman.

CHAPTER V
A BABY LOST AND RECOVERED

In the scouting of that morning Truman Flagg took an active part, and he alone of all who were out discovered the trail of the fleeing Ottawas. Following it far enough to assure himself that no unfriendly forest ranger had run across it, he turned his steps in the direction of the Seneca village. Here, although he was received with a certain coolness, arising from his participation in the incident of the previous evening, no affront was offered him, and he had no difficulty in acquiring the information he desired. Thus he was able to report to Major Hester, on his return to Tawtry House, that Mahng not only lived, but was in a fair way to recover from his injury, and that by means of swift runners the grievance of the Indians had already been laid before Sir William Johnson.

This report was confirmed on the following day, by the appearance of a delegation of Seneca chiefs, who brought a note from the governor, and demanded that Major Hester deliver to them the Ottawa captive. Sir William's note, though extremely courteous, was very firm, and contained an unmistakable order for restoration to the Senecas of their lawful prisoner. It also chided the major for interfering between Indians, at a risk of disturbing the friendly relations between the English and their Iroquois neighbors.

With the reading of this note an angry flush mantled the soldier's bronzed cheeks, and he seemed on the point of expressing his feelings in forcible language. Controlling himself with a visible effort, and bidding Truman Flagg interpret his words, he replied to the chiefs as follows:--

"Brothers: I have listened to your demand and find it a just one. The talking-paper of the white chief bids me deliver to you a prisoner known as Songa the Ottawa. The orders of the white chief must be obeyed, as I would obey this one were it possible to do so, but it is not. Listen. As I walked before my lodge, a stranger, whom I had never seen, ran from the forest and fell at my feet. He was bleeding from many wounds, and exhausted from long running. An enemy followed, and sought to kill him; when my son, a little child, threw himself across the stranger's neck and saved his life. Was not that a sign from the Great Spirit that he wished the stranger to live? Could I do less than was done by that little child? You know I could not. You know that no Seneca warrior would allow a man to be killed who sought his protection in such a manner. So I lifted this stranger and took him to my lodge. At the same time I told his enemy that I would keep him until an order could be brought from the great white chief for him to be delivered up. Now you have brought that order, and, were the stranger still in my lodge, I would deliver him to you; but he is not. He left me that same night. How, I know not. He was sore wounded, and was lodged in a secure place, but in the morning he was gone. I am told that he is a medicine man of the Metai. May he not have been removed by the magic of his circle? No matter. He was here and is gone. You look to me for him, and I cannot produce him. That is all. I have spoken."

A dignified old Seneca chief arose to reply, and said; "We have heard the words of my white brother, and we believe them to be true, for his tongue is not crooked. He alone of all white men has never lied to us. He says the prisoner is gone, and it must be so. But it is not well. Our hearts are heavy at the escape of so brave a captive. What, then, will my brother give us in his place, that the heaviness of our hearts may be lifted?"

"I will give you," replied Major Hester, "two guns, and ten red blankets, twenty pounds of powder and fifty pounds of lead, one piece of blue cloth, one piece of red cloth, and five pounds of tobacco. Is it enough?"

"It is enough," answered the chief, while the eyes of his companions glistened at the prospect of this munificent present. "But," he continued, "there was a woman. What will my brother give for her?"

"Nothing," answered the white brother, promptly, "for she was not your prisoner."

"Ugh!" grunted the Indians.

"There is also Mahng," continued the savage diplomat, whose rule of action was that of his white colleagues in the same service; namely, to give as little and get as much as possible. "What will my brother give him to help the healing of his wounds?"

"I will give Mahng a handsome present whenever he shall come to receive it, that there may be no bad blood between us," was the answer; and with these concessions the Indians expressed themselves as well content.

The proprietor of Tawtry House kept his word in regard to the presents; but Mahng never came to claim those set apart for him. Instead of so doing, he sent word to Major Hester that no gift, save that of his life's blood, would ever atone for the insult of that kick, nor wipe out the enmity between them.

"So be it, then, if he will have it so," replied the soldier, with a light laugh, when this was reported to him; but his wife turned pale and trembled as she recalled the undying hate expressed by Mahng's scowling face. Nor was the Ojibwa's threat an entirely idle one, as the settlers discovered to their sorrow, when several of their cattle were killed, an outbuilding was burned, and finally the major himself had a narrow escape with his life, from a shot fired by an unseen foe. Finally, these things became so annoying that Sir William Johnson notified the Senecas to drive Mahng from their country, or hand him over to the whites for punishment, unless they wished to forfeit the valuable annual present, sent to them by their great Father of England, an instalment of which was then due.

As the Diver was by no means popular in his adopted tribe, he was promptly carried across the Niagara river, and forbidden ever to set foot on its eastern shore again, under penalty of death. Having performed this virtuous act, the Senecas moved eastward to the long council-house of the Six Nations, which was located in the country of the Onondagas, where they were to receive their presents and share in the deliberations of their confederacy.

It was two months after the incidents above described, and several weeks had passed without an Indian having been seen in the vicinity of Tawtry House. So absolutely peaceful were its surroundings that the vigilance of its inmates was relaxed, and during the daytime, at least, they came and went at will, without a thought of insecurity.

This peace was rudely broken one morning by shrill cries from the Scotch nurse maid who, an hour before, had strolled with her infant charge toward the lake. She now ran to the house in an agony of terror, and uttering unintelligible screams. It was at first believed that the child was drowned, but finally the distracted parents gleaned from the girl's half-coherent words that she had left him in safety at some distance from the shore, for a single minute, while she stepped to the water's edge for a drink. When she returned he had disappeared, nor was there any answer to her calling.

For two days search parties scoured the surrounding forest, but without avail. There was not an experienced trailer among them, Truman Flagg being with Sir William Johnson at the Onondaga council-house. Toward the close of the second day, while Major Hester and most of his men were still engaged in their fruitless search, the heartbroken mother walked listlessly to the place where her child had last been seen. She had already been there many times, unconsciously, but irresistibly attracted to the spot.

On this occasion, as she was about to turn back, there came to her ear the cry of an infant. Like a tigress robbed of her young, and with blazing eyes, the bereaved woman sprang in the direction of the sound, and in another instant her child, alive and well, was clasped to her bosom. He had been hidden beneath the low-spreading branches of a small cedar, and she snatched him from a bark cradle, exquisitely made and lined with costly furs.

Like one pursued by a great terror, she fled to the house with her precious burden, nor would she permit one to take it from her until her husband's return.

When they examined the child they found him without scratch or blemish, save for a curious and inflamed disfiguration on his left arm, just below the shoulder. Though this soon healed, it was long before its mystery was explained; but when Truman Flagg saw it, he pronounced it to be the tattooed mark of an Indian totem.

CHAPTER VI
THE WILDERNESS

In a new country the changes effected during sixteen years are apt to be greater than those of a lifetime in long-established communities. Certainly this was the case in North America during the sixteen years immediately preceding that of 1763. The bitter fighting between England and France for the supremacy of the new world that began with the signal defeat of the English army under Braddock, in 1755, was ended four years later by Wolfe's decisive victory on the Plains of Abraham. A year later France retired from the conflict and surrendered Canada, with all its dependencies, to the English. These dependencies included a long chain of tiny forts, about some of which were clustered thrifty French settlements that extended entirely around the Great Lakes and south of them into the valley of the Ohio. Among these were Niagara at the mouth of the river of that name, Presque Isle on the site of the present city of Erie, Sandusky, Detroit, Mackinac, Fort Howard on Green Bay, and Fort St. Joseph near the southern end of Lake Michigan. While from its commanding position the most important of these forts was the first named; the largest, and the one surrounded by the most thriving settlement was at Detroit. Here the fort itself was a palisaded village of one hundred compactly built houses standing on the western bank of the Detroit river. Beyond it, on both sides for nearly eight miles, stretched the prosperous settlement of French peasants, whose long, narrow farms reached far back from the river, though in every case the tidy white houses and outbuildings stood close to the water's edge.

The English settlements at the close of the war with France had not crossed the Alleghanies, and in the province of New York the western bank of the Hudson was an almost unbroken wilderness. Through the country of the Six Nations, and by their especial permission, a military route, guarded by a line of forts, had been established, though it was clearly understood by the Indians that all these should be abandoned as soon as the war was ended. This route began at the frontier town of Albany. Here the traveller left the clumsy but comfortable sloop on board which he had perhaps spent a week or more on the voyage from New York, and embarked in a canoe or flat-boat, which was laboriously poled against the swift current of the Mohawk river. Thus he passed the old Dutch town of Schenectady, Johnson Hall and Johnson Castle, Forts Hunter and Herkimer, and at length reached the head of river navigation at Fort Stanwix. From here a short portage through the forest led him to the waters of Wood creek, where he might again embark and float with the sluggish current to the Royal Blockhouse on the shore of Oneida lake. Crossing this, and passing under the walls of Port Brewerton at the source of the Oswego river, he would descend the swift waters of that stream to Fort Oswego on the shore of Lake Ontario. From here his course in any direction lay over the superb waterways of the great inland lakes whose open navigation was only interrupted by a toilsome portage around the great cataract of the Niagara river.

Beyond these few isolated dots of white settlements and the slender lines of communication between them, the whole vast interior country was buried in the shade of an unbroken forest that swept like a billowy sea of verdure over plains, hills, valleys, and mountains, screening the sunlight from innumerable broad rivers and rushing streams, and spreading its leafy protection over uncounted millions of beasts, birds, and fishes. Here dwelt the Indian, and before the coming of the white man the forest supplied all his simple needs. Its gloomy mazes were threaded in every direction by his trails, deep-trodden by the feet of many generations, and forming a network of communication between all villages and places of importance. So carefully did these narrow highways follow lines of shortest distance and easiest grade, that when the white man began to lay out his own roads he could do no better than adopt their suggestions.

With the coming of the whites, the life of the Indian was subjected to sudden and radical changes. Having learned of the existence and use of guns, knives, kettles, blankets, and innumerable other things that appealed to his savage notions of comfort and utility, he must now have them, and for them would trade furs. So the fur traders became important features of the forest life, and their business grew to be so immensely profitable that its control was one of the prime objects for which England and France fought in America. The little forts that the French scattered over the country were only trading-posts, and at them, so long as their builders ruled, the Indians were treated with a fairness and courtesy that won their firm friendship and made them stanch allies in times of war. But when the French power was broken, and the Indians, without at all understanding why, found that they must hereafter deal only with English fur traders, all this was changed.

There was no longer a war on hand nor a rival power in the land, therefore the necessity for conciliating the Indian and gaining his friendship no longer existed. The newcomers did not care so much for furs as they did for land. For this they were willing to trade rum, but not guns, knives, powder, or bullets. These must be kept from the Indian, lest he do mischief. He no longer found in the white man a friend, but a master, and a very cruel one at that.

It was now considered good economy to withhold the presents that in war time had been so lavishly bestowed on the Indians, and the one problem that the English sought to solve was how to get rid of the undesirable red man as cheaply and quickly as possible. The little trading-posts, in which he had been made a welcome guest, were now filled with red-coated soldiers, who called him a dog and treated him as such. He became ragged and hungry, was driven from the homes of his fathers, and finally began to perceive that even the privilege of living was not to be granted him much longer. He grew desperate, and his hatred against those who had driven away his kind French friends and brought about all his present misery became very bitter. He saw plainly that if he did not drive these redcoats back to the sea whence they came, they would soon sweep his race from the face of the earth. There seemed to be only a few white men and many Indians; but while the former were united under one great leader, the latter were divided into many tribes with many little leaders. If they, too, would only find some great chief, under whom all the tribes could unite, how quickly would they wipe out the hated redcoats and teach the English to respect their rights. Perhaps as soon as they began to fight for themselves the white-coated soldiers of France would come again to help them. At any rate, certain white men told them this would happen, and they were believed. If only they could find a leader!

Gradually, but with convincing proof, it dawned upon the unhappy Indians that a great leader had arisen among them, and was ready to deal the decisive blow that should set them free. To tribe after tribe and to village after village came messengers bearing broad belts of wampum and the crimson hatchet of war. They came in the name of Pontiac, war chief of the fierce Ottawas, head medicine man of the powerful Metai, friend of Montcalm, stanch ally of the French during the recent war, and leader of his people at the battle of the Monongahela, where stubborn Braddock was slain with his redcoats, and even the dreaded "long-knives" from Virginia were forced to fly.

Far and wide travelled the messengers of this mighty chieftain, and everywhere was his war hatchet eagerly accepted. Far and wide went Pontiac himself, and wherever his burning words were heard the children of the forest became crazed with the fever of war. Finally, the fierce plan was perfected. The blow was to be struck at every British post west of Niagara on the same day. With the fall of these, the triumphant forest hordes were to rush against the settlements and visit upon them the same cruel destruction that had overtaken their own villages whenever the white man had seen fit to wipe them from his patch.

While this movement had gained ground until the fatal storm was just ready to burst, it had been conducted with such secrecy that only one white man even suspected its existence, and his name was Graham Hester.

CHAPTER VII
THE MAJOR RE-ENTERS ACTIVE SERVICE

On the breaking out of the French war, Major Hester accepted his friend's invitation to remove his family to Johnson Hall, and make that his home during the troublous times that would render Tawtry House an unsafe place of residence. This he did the more readily on account of his wife's health, which was so precarious that, while the major was confident he could defend his forest fortress against any ordinary attack, he feared lest the excitement of such an affair might prove too much for the frail woman who was dearer to him than life.

Alas for his precautions! During the wearisome eastward journey, the travellers were drenched by a fierce storm of rain and hail that was followed by a chilling wind. So furious was the tempest that it was impossible to wholly protect the invalid from it, and in less than a week thereafter the noisy bustle of Johnson Hall was silenced for an hour by her funeral. So deeply did the rugged soldier feel his loss, that he vowed he would never again set foot in the house that had been hers, and that, as soon as he could make provision for his children, he would seek in battle for the king, that reunion with his loved one that death alone could grant.

The children thus deprived of a mother's tender care were Donald, now a sturdy lad of twelve years, and Edith, a dainty little maiden two years younger. The former was wise beyond his years in forest lore, which he had eagerly imbibed from the tuition of that master of woodcraft, Truman Flagg. At the same time he was sadly deficient in a knowledge of books and many other things that go to make up the education of a gentleman. Him, therefore, the major decided to send to New York to be fitted for the college then known as "King's," but afterwards famous under the name of "Columbia."

Against this decision the lad raised strenuous objections, declaring that his sole ambition was to become a soldier, and that such a one could learn to fight without the aid of books.

"True, my son, so he can, after a fashion," replied the major, gravely. "But, in the art of war, as in every other art, all our teachings come from those who have preceded us, and the most important of these are recorded in the books they have left for our consideration. Again, as the soldier of to-day is the modern representative of the chivalrous knight of olden time, he must needs be a gentleman, and an uneducated gentleman would be as sorry a spectacle as an unarmed soldier in battle. So, my dear boy, accept thy fate kindly and make a soldier's fight against the enemy named ignorance. Upon the day of thy graduation from King's College, if my influence can compass it, which I doubt not it can, a commission in one of His Majesty's American regiments shall await thy acceptance. I shall send our little lass with thee, and both she and thyself will be entertained in the household of Madam Rothsay, the widow of a dear friend of mine, who has agreed to receive you and fulfil, so far as may be, a mother's duty toward my motherless children."

The major escorted his children as far as Albany, where he embarked them, together with the Scotch nurse who had cared for both of them from their birth, on board a packet-sloop that should carry them to their new house. Having thus made provision for the welfare of his dear ones, the lonely man proceeded to fulfil the destiny he had planned by joining as a volunteer aid the army which, under General Johnson, was charged with the capture of Crown Point on Lake Champlain. In this campaign it was largely owing to Major Hester's soldierly knowledge and tactical skill that the French army, under Baron Dieskau, which had advanced as far as the southern end of Lake George, was defeated. For this victory Sir William Johnson was raised to a baronetcy and presented with a purse of five thousand pounds.

Through the war Major Hester fought with one army or another, always in the forefront of battle, as he was a leader in council; but never finding the boon of death which he craved. At length he stood with Wolfe on the lofty Plain of Abraham, and in the fall of Quebec witnessed the fatal blow to French power in America. In all this time he had never returned to the forest house that he had last looked upon in company with his beloved wife. Whether his resolution not to visit it would have lived to the end can never be known, for in the second year of the war a marauding party from an army, which, under Montcalm, had just captured and destroyed Oswego, reached Tawtry House and burned it to the ground.

After the surrender of Canada, Major Hester visited his children in New York City. Here he found his boy, grown almost beyond recognition, domiciled in the new King's College building, then just completed, and doing well in his studies, but keenly regretting that the war was ended without his participation. The white-haired soldier also found his daughter, Edith, now fifteen years of age, budding into a beautiful womanhood, and bearing so strong a resemblance to her mother that he gazed at her with mixed emotions of pain and delight.

During his stay in the city, the major was frequently consulted upon military affairs by the English commander-in-chief, Sir Jeffry Amherst, who finally begged him to accompany the expedition which he was about to send into the far west, under the redoubtable Colonel Rogers, of ranger fame, to receive the surrender of the more distant French posts.

"Rogers is impetuous, and needs a man of your experience to serve as a balance-wheel," said Sir Jeffry. "Besides, I want some one of your ability and knowledge of Indian affairs to take command of Detroit, the principal settlement and most important trading-post in the west. So, Hester, if you will accept this duty, you will not only be serving the king, but doing me a great personal favor as well."

Willing to continue for a while longer in active service, and having no other plan, Major Hester accepted Sir Jeffry's offer, and set forth on his long journey, joining Rogers at Fort Niagara, where, with the aid of cranes and ox-teams, the rangers were laboriously transporting their heavy whale-boats over the steep portage around the great cataract.

At length the little flotilla was again launched, and as it skirted the southern shore of Lake Erie, its every movement was watched by the keen eyes of Indian scouts, concealed in dense forest coverts, and reported in detail to the chief of that country; for never before had a body of British troops ventured so far into the interior. Finally, in one of their camps the rangers were visited by an imposing array of Indian sachems, headed by the great chief himself, who demanded the reason of their presence in his country.

When Rogers, in reply, had stated the nature of his business, the chief began a speech, in which he forbade the further advance of the English. Suddenly his eye rested upon Major Hester, who had just left his tent to attend the council. The speech of the Indian came to an abrupt pause, and gazing fixedly at the white-haired officer, he inquired if he were not the chief who dwelt in the great house of the two trees in the land of the Senecas.

"I did dwell there," replied the major, greatly surprised at the question.

"Does my brother of the two-tree house wish to journey through the country of the Ottawas?" demanded the chieftain.

"Certainly, I do," was the reply.

"For peace or for war?" queried the savage, laconically.

"For peace," answered Major Hester. "The war is ended, and we do but journey to take peaceable possession of those forts which the French have given over to the English."

"Ugh! It is good! Let my white brother travel in peace, for Pontiac knows that his tongue is straight, and that what he says must be true words."

With this the haughty chieftain, followed by his savage retinue, left the camp, and not another Indian was seen until Detroit was reached, though, as was afterwards learned, a strong body of Pontiac's warriors had awaited them at the mouth of the Detroit river, and were only restrained from attacking the flotilla by their leader's express command.

Neither Major Hester nor Colonel Rogers knew what to make of this curious behavior on the part of the powerful Indian who had evidently been determined to oppose their progress. The former could not recall ever having seen him or held intercourse with him, though, after he assumed command of Fort Detroit, Pontiac paid him frequent visits, and always evinced a strong friendship for the honest

At War with Pontiac

soldier, who invariably treated him and his people with consideration and fairness. Frequently, too, Pontiac complained to the major of the outrages perpetrated by other English commanders, their brutal soldiers, and the horde of reckless traders who swarmed through the country. He declared that if they were continued, the Indians would rise against their oppressors and sweep them from the face of the earth.

Fully appreciating the state of affairs, but powerless to alter it for the better, save in his own jurisdiction, Major Hester appealed to Sir William Johnson, begging him to visit the western country and use his powerful influence to quiet the growing discontent. This Sir William did with great pomp and ceremony in 1761, finding himself just in time to quell, by lavish presents and still more lavish promises, a general uprising of the Algonquin tribes. The peaceful relations thus established lasted but a short time, however, and within a year the aggressions of the whites had become more pronounced, and the situation of the Indians more desperate than ever. Pontiac had disappeared from the vicinity of Detroit, and for many months Major Hester had not seen him. At the same time he was well informed of the cruelties practised upon the natives, and foresaw that they could not much longer be restrained from retaliating in their own bloody fashion. Being unwilling to fight on the side of injustice and oppression, he at length prayed Sir Jeffry Amherst to relieve him from his command. This request was granted, and late in 1762 he was succeeded by Major Gladwyn, an officer with a brave record as a fighter and unhampered by any troublesome consideration of the rights or wrongs of Indians. Although thus relieved of his command, certain duties arose to detain Major Hester for several months at Detroit; and the momentous spring of 1763 found him still an inmate of that frontier post.

CHAPTER VIII
DONALD SETS FORTH ON A PERILOUS MISSION

No rising sun ever witnessed a fairer scene than that presented by the little wilderness settlement of Detroit on the sixth of May, 1763. All nature was rejoicing in the advent of spring and donning its livery of green. The broad river, flowing southward with a mighty volume of water from four inland seas of which it formed the sole outlet, was lined as far as the eye could reach with the white houses and fertile fields of French farmers. From these, spirals of blue smoke curled peacefully, and the voices of cattle answered each other in morning greetings. A darker mass of buildings on the western bank denoted the palisaded village in which dwelt the British garrison, their wives and children, and some fifty fur traders, with their Canadian employees. The houses within the palisades, about one hundred in number, were mostly low, wooden structures, roofed with bark or thatch. The village was square in form, and while one side opened on the river, the other three were enclosed by wooden walls, twenty-five feet in height, with log bastions at the corners, and a blockhouse over each of the three gateways. Several pieces of light artillery were mounted on the bastions, and anchored in the river lay the armed schooners and . At some distance from the fort, both up and down the river, rose the smoke of populous Indian villages, for all the natives of that section were in from their winter hunting, and gathered at this point for trade. Over the placid waters light canoes occasionally darted from bank to bank. A boat brigade, bound for the far north, was just starting from the fort, and the Canadian voyageurs, gay with fringes, beads, and crimson sashes, caused the morning air to ring with a tuneful chorus as boat after boat shot away and stemmed the current with lusty oars.

Not far from the point of this noisy embarkation was another, though much less ostentatious scene of departure and leave-taking. In the stern of a birch canoe, paddle in hand and evidently impatient to be off, sat one of Rogers' buckskin-clad rangers, who was about to revisit his distant New Hampshire home, for the first time in three years. Near by, on the strand, stood two men, both tall and possessed of a military bearing. One, who wore the undress uniform of an officer, was elderly and white-haired, while the other, slender, and clad much as was the ranger in the canoe, was in the first flush of splendid young manhood. As these two stood hand in hand, the younger said: "Can I not persuade you, father, even at this last moment, to change your mind and accompany us? Poor Edith will be so dreadfully disappointed."

"I fear she will, Donald," returned Major Hester, with a sad smile, "but as this life is mainly composed of disappointments, the sooner she learns to bear them with composure, the better. I had indeed looked forward to taking this journey with you, to clasping my dear girl in my arms once more, and ere the year was ended to rebuilding Tawtry House, in which to establish her as mistress. With the war ended, I fondly hoped that a certain degree of happiness were still possible to me, and looked forward to securing it by some such means as I have just outlined."

"And is it not, father?" broke in the youth, eagerly. "Surely you have done far more than your duty here, and--"

"No man has done that, Donald, so long as there remains an unperformed task for which he is fitted," interrupted Major Hester, gravely. "So long as I believe a crisis in Indian affairs to be imminent, and that by remaining here I may be able to avert it, at least until the reinforcements which it is now yours to hasten can arrive, it is clearly my duty to stay. So off with you, lad. Don't run any risks that can just as well be avoided, and don't try to avoid any that, if successfully taken, will serve to speed your errand. Farewell, my son. May God bless you and keep you and bring your enterprise to a happy termination."

After the canoe had departed, Major Hester ascended one of the water bastions, where he watched it until it became a tiny speck, and finally vanished behind the projecting land then known as Montreal point.

Donald Hester had striven so manfully with his studies that he was finally graduated from King's College, well toward the head of his class, during the previous summer. Thereupon he had been rewarded with his heart's desire, an ensign's commission in the Royal Americans. To the new and fascinating duties of his chosen profession he at once devoted himself with such ardor as to draw favorable comment from his superiors. After serving at several posts he had, to his great delight, been transferred to Detroit, where the soldier father and soldier son, each more than proud of the other, were joyfully reunited after their years of separation. Here, too, he renewed his boyhood's intimacy with forest life, and eagerly resumed his long-neglected studies in wilderness lore, and woodcraft.

Although Donald was generally liked by his brother officers, he had no taste for the dissipations with which they sought to relieve the monotony of their lives. In place of these, he chose to take gun or fishing-rod and go off on long excursions in his canoe. On one of these occasions, when far down the river and in vigorous pursuit of a wounded duck, he had the misfortune to break his only paddle short off. In a moment he was helplessly drifting with the powerful current toward the open waters of Lake Erie. In this dilemma, his only resource was to paddle with his hands, and attempt by this tedious method to force his craft to the nearest shore. While he was thus awkwardly engaged, there came it ripple of laughter from close beside him, and he started up just in time to gaze squarely into the laughing face of an Indian girl, who instantly impressed him as the most graceful creature he had ever seen. She occupied, with a girl companion, a beautifully painted and ornamented canoe, which had slipped up to him with the lightness of a thistle-down. As the young soldier caught sight of her she was in the very act of tossing a paddle into his own helpless craft.

Then the strange canoe darted away like an arrow, while the only answer to the young man's fervently expressed thanks was a merry peal of laughter, coupled with an exclamation, of which he caught but the single word "ah-mo." These were wafted back to him as the flying canoe disappeared behind the point of a small island. With a desire to learn something more of the bewitching forest maiden, who had come so opportunely to his aid, Donald urged his own craft vigorously in that direction, but when he rounded the point there was no trace to be seen of those whom he sought.

So deep an impression had the olive-tinted face, the laughing eyes, and the jetty tresses of the girl who tossed the paddle to him made upon the young ensign, that they haunted both his sleeping and his wakeful hours; but, plan as he might, he could not succeed in seeing her again, nor did his cautiously worded inquiries serve to elicit the slightest information concerning her.

Perhaps it was well for the efficiency of the service that about this time Major Gladwyn selected Donald to be the bearer of certain despatches to Sir William Johnson, concerning the reinforcements and supplies that he expected to receive by the spring brigade of boats from Niagara. Major Hester, who had intended to return East about this time, suddenly decided to remain at Detroit a while longer. He therefore intrusted a number of private despatches to the young courier, both for Sir William and General Amherst. Besides its more important despatches, Donald's canoe was freighted with a large packet of letters from members of the garrison to distant friends and loved ones. Thus it set forth on its long and perilous voyage followed by fond hopes and best wishes from every member of the band of exiles left behind.

CHAPTER IX
ST. AUBIN'S STARTLING INFORMATION

When Major Hester slowly and thoughtfully returned to his quarters after witnessing the departure of his son, he found sitting on the doorstep, and patiently awaiting his coming, a Canadian woman. Beside her stood her stolid-looking husband, whom the major recognized as a well-to-do farmer of the settlement, to whom he had granted some trifling favors while in command of the post.

"Good-morning, madame. Good-morning, St. Aubin. To what am I indebted for the honor of this early call? What can I do for you?" asked the old soldier, in answer to the humble salutations with which they greeted his approach.

"Ah! monsieur, we have come," began the woman.

"Certainment, we have come," echoed her husband.

"Jean!"

"Pardon, Marie."

"We have come with despair on account of the previous abounding kindness of monsieur, to divulge him--"

"A secret! A secret terrible!" exploded the old man, who was nervously standing first on one foot and then on the other.

"Jean!"

"Oui, Marie."

"If you have an important secret to confide, had we not better enter the house?" suggested the major, who saw from the excited earnestness of the worthy couple that something very unusual had occurred to agitate them.

They accepted this invitation, and the major finally gleaned from their combined and interjectory statements that on the previous day Madame St. Aubin, visiting the Ottawa village, had surprised a number of warriors in the act of cutting off the long barrels of their guns, until the entire length of each weapon was not more than a yard. Moreover, she had overheard an Indian who was somewhat under the influence of liquor boast that ere many days he would have English scalps with which to fringe his leggings.

"Has any one else seen these things or noted symptoms of uneasiness among the Indians?" demanded the major.

"Yes. Basil, the blacksmith, has been troubled for days by Indians begging for loans of files and saws, for what purpose they would not state."

"But why do you not carry this matter to Major Gladwyn, who is in command, instead of to me, who now possess no authority?"

"Because, monsieur, the commandant makes of us a jest and cares not to listen. Aussi, because we care not for him; but to you, monsieur, who have formerly turned many of our sorrows into joys, we wish not that harm should come. For ourselves, we have no fear. The savages will not harm the French. But for the English, whom they love not--well, there it is different."

"You think, then, that the fort is in danger?"

"Of an attack, monsieur. Yes."

"How soon?"

"Who can tell? Perhaps in one week. Perhaps even to-morrow."

"Will you come again this evening, before the gates are closed, and bring any further information you may gain during the day?"

"We dare not, monsieur. All the French are now too closely watched. This morning we sell eggs. In the evening it would be known that we had no business."

"If I leave the post an hour after sunset and walk just beyond the church, will you meet me there and deliver to me your information?"

"If it is possible, we will; for the thing that monsieur demands must be granted on account of his, ofttimes of the heart, kindness."

After the departure of these people, Major Hester thoughtfully made his way to the quarters of the commanding officer, whom he found at breakfast.

Gladwyn, though a brave man and a thorough soldier, was a high liver, inclined to dissipation, impatient of advice, and held an undisguised contempt for all Indians. To crown all, he was extremely jealous of the ascendancy over the native tribes gained by his predecessor in command, whom he cordially disliked and wished out of the way. On the present occasion he greeted him in courteous terms, but coldly and without rising.

"This is indeed an early call, major. I suppose I am indebted for the pleasure to the fact that Ensign Hester took an early departure, according to instructions, and your paternal instinct led you to speed his journey. I must confess my surprise that you did not accompany him. I suppose you are waiting for the opportunity of a more comfortable passage by schooner. For my part, I prefer the excitement of a canoe voyage; but I suppose as one grows old--"

"A soldier never grows so old as to forget his duty, Major Gladwyn," answered the elder officer, stiffly. "And I can assure you that only a strong sense of duty causes me to linger in a place where my presence is so evidently undesirable. But I have not interrupted your breakfast for the purpose of discussing personalities. I desire to lay before you a bit of information that has just come to my knowledge, regarding certain suspicious movements among the Indians, who, as you must be aware, are gathered about the post in unusual numbers. They are cutting off their gun-barrels to such a length that the weapons may be concealed beneath their blankets. I have this direct from St. Aubin, whose wife, visiting the Ottawa village yesterday, discovered its inmates to be thus engaged."

"It must have been an interesting sight," replied Gladwyn, carelessly, "but I fail to perceive what possible interest it can have for me. I suppose the rascals have learned that they can shoot just as effectively, or rather as ineffectively, with short gun-barrels as with long, and so have wisely decided to do away with useless weight. By Jove, Hester, I have laughed more than once at the shrewdness of our traders who sell cheap flint-lock muskets to the redskins for as many otter or beaver skins as can be piled between stock and muzzle, and have these trade guns built with an increased length each year. Rather clever, is it not?"

"It is a bit of infamous cheating that will sooner or later recoil on our own heads," replied the other, hotly. "But that is neither here nor there. The question is, whether or not the Indians mean to attack this post, and whether it is prepared for an attack in case they do?"

"If they only would, my dear sir, I for one should welcome it as a cheerful break in the deadly monotony of our lives in this forsaken place. As for preparations, you should be among the last to question that the troops of His Most Gracious Majesty of England are always prepared to meet any number of naked savages under any circumstances."

"That was Braddock's opinion," remarked Major Hester, grimly, "and he paid for it with his life. But granting that we are able to withstand an attack, are we prepared for a siege?"

"Oh come, major!" exclaimed Gladwyn, rather testily, "that question is rather a severe test of one's credulity. As if it were possible for a parcel of howling redskins to conduct a siege! No one knows better than you that their only method of fighting is a surprise, a yell, a volley, and then a retreat. They are absolutely incapable of sustained effort."

"Are you acquainted with Pontiac, the present war chief of the united tribes?" inquired Major Hester, coldly.

"Certainly I am, and a more conceited, ignorant, boastful, treacherous, cowardly, and utterly worthless bit of red humanity than he I have yet to meet. I have already warned him away from this section of country, and if he persists in remaining where he is so little wanted, I shall be obliged to teach him a lesson."

"Very well, major, if these are your unalterable opinions regarding the present state of affairs, I have nothing more to say, save to wish you a very good morning," replied the elder officer, as he turned to leave. "However," he added, "I shall still consider it my duty to report any further bits of information that may come to me."

"While thanking you, I beg you not to inconvenience yourself to do so," remarked Gladwyn, frigidly, and with this the interview ended.

That evening, while a dull glow still lingered in the western sky, though the shadows of dusk were fallen on the fort and its surroundings, Major Hester passed the sentry at one of the gates and walked slowly, as though for an aimless stroll, as far as the little French-Canadian church. On reaching it he detected a dim figure in its shadow and asked in a low tone, "Is that you, St. Aubin?"

"No, monsieur," was the answer, in a girl's voice, "but I am his daughter, and am come in his place, as he is detained by company. He bade me deliver a message to you alone and then hasten back." With this the girl almost whispered in the ear of the old soldier a few words that caused his teeth to clench and his heartstrings to tighten. She had hardly concluded, when an approaching step from the direction of the fort caused her to spring aside and fly with the swiftness of a deer.

"Who goes there?" challenged Major Hester.

"Pardon me, major," answered the well-known voice of the commandant. "I had no idea I was interrupting a tete-a-tete. In fact, I did not associate you with trysts of this kind."

"That will do, Major Gladwyn," interrupted the other, sternly. "I have but this minute learned that on the morrow Pontiac, with sixty of his warriors, all having guns concealed beneath their blankets, will demand to hold a council with you. The leader will make a speech, at the conclusion of which he will present a belt of wampum. Your taking of that belt will be the signal for a general massacre of every English soul within the limits of Fort Detroit, save only the one to whom the chief has presented his calumet."

"Do you believe this cock-and-bull story, Hester?" demanded the startled commander.

"Even now is the war dance in progress," was the reply. "Listen!"

At that moment a waft of night air bore to their ears the sullen booming of distant war drums and the wild chorus of quavering yells with which the frenzied savages across the river greeted Pontiac's declaration of war against the hated English.

"By Heaven, Hester! I believe you are right," cried Gladwyn, as he listened to these ominous sounds. "At any rate, I will accept your warning, and make such preparations as will show those devils that we are not to be caught napping."

CHAPTER X
PONTIAC DECLARES WAR

Although Gladwyn caused half of his force to be kept under arms that night, and doubled his sentries, nothing occurred to disturb the settlement. In the morning, as the rising sun dispelled the fleecy mist-clouds from above the river, a fleet of canoes was seen crossing from the eastern shore. These effected a landing at some distance above the fort, and soon afterwards the wide, open common behind it was animated by the presence of hundreds of Indians. There were stately warriors in paint and blankets, young braves stripped to the waist-cloth for a game of ball, maidens whose cheeks were ruddy with vermilion, robed in embroidered and beaded garments of fawn skin, and naked children, frolicking like so many puppies.

Save in the occasional scowling face and preoccupied air of some dark-browed warrior, and a slow but noticeable gathering of these near the principal gate of the fort, there was nothing to arouse suspicion or indicate that these visitors had any save the most friendly feelings toward the whites.

Pontiac having sent word to Major Gladwyn that he desired to meet the white chief in council, about ten o'clock the Indian leader and some sixty of his principal men were seen approaching in single file from the direction of the bridge across Parent's creek, a mile and a half north of the fort. As they drew near the great gateway, it was noticed that in spite of the heat of the day every warrior was wrapped to the chin in his gayly colored blanket. The faces of all were streaked with ochre, vermilion, white, and black paint, while from their scalp-locks depended plumes of eagle, hawk, or turkey feathers, indicative of their rank or prowess in battle.

As the great gate was swung open to admit this barbaric procession, they entered the fort with stately tread and in grave silence, led by the mighty chief, who, with proudly lifted head and flashing eyes, looked every inch a forest king. Suddenly he started, uttered a deep ejaculation, and half turned as though to retreat. On either side of the street down which he must pass to the council-house was drawn up a motionless line of red-coated soldiers. Above them their fixed bayonets glinted ominously in the bright sunlight. Behind them every house was closed, and at the street corners stood groups of stalwart fur traders, surrounded by their half-savage employees, all armed to the teeth. In all these rigid figures there was a grim air of determination, though no sound was to be heard save the measured throbbing of an unseen drum.

It is no wonder that Pontiac started. In a single glance he saw that he had been betrayed and that his plan was known. Still, his hesitation was but momentary and hardly noticed ere with immobile face he resumed his march toward the great council-house that stood near the water's edge, on the further side of the town. As the procession of fierce warriors, decked in the fullest glory of savage habiliment, moved slowly down the street, frightened faces gazed furtively at them from behind half-closed blinds, while the regular tap of the unseen drum seemed to assume an angrier tone, as though impatient to break forth in the furious rattle of a "charge."

In the council-house the Indians found Gladwyn and his officers seated in a semicircle at the upper end, waiting to receive them. They also noted that each

At War with Pontiac

of these, besides being in full uniform, wore his sword and a brace of pistols. At this additional evidence of the discovery of their design, and that they had placed themselves completely within the enemy's power, the warriors exchanged uneasy glances, and seemed inclined to make a rush for the door rather than seat themselves on the mats prepared for them.

"Why," demanded Pontiac, "do I see so many of my white brother's young men standing outside with guns in their hands?"

Gladwyn replied that it was customary for his soldiers to go through with an armed drill every day.

When the Indians were finally seated, one of them filled, lighted, and handed to Pontiac the great chief's own superb calumet. Its red stone bowl, which held a quarter of a pound of tobacco, was carved with rare skill, and its long stem was curiously inlaid with shell-work, besides being ornamented with quills and feathers. After each member of the council, white as well as red, beginning with Gladwyn, had slowly drawn a whiff from this mighty calumet, and it came again to Pontiac, he rose and said:--

"In token of the peace which I desire shall always exist between the red man and his white brother I now present this pipe to these friends, that they may keep it forever. That its message may be heard with open ears, I deliver it to the care of the oldest among you, to him whose hair is white with the wisdom of many years."

Thus saying, the chief stepped forward and laid the gorgeous calumet across the knees of Major Hester, while a grunt of approbation came from the throats of those behind him. Gladwyn, who alone of the assembled whites knew the meaning of this act, cast a startled and suspicious glance at the veteran soldier thus singled out for some other fate than death, while the recipient himself was noticeably embarrassed by the incident.

But the attention of all was immediately occupied by other things. Holding a splendid belt of wampum in his hands, Pontiac was now addressing Gladwyn with the eloquence for which he was so justly famed. He recounted the many outrages suffered by his people at the hands of the English, and especially their fur traders. Against these he demanded protection. He spoke for nearly an hour, during which time his every gesture was keenly watched by the English officers, who feared that in spite of their precautions he might still attempt some desperate move.

Pontiac was in a dilemma. It was customary at the close of a speech to present the belt of wampum, which the speaker always held, to him who was expected to reply. To omit this formality would be equivalent to a declaration of war. It had been understood that his followers were to fall upon the English officers the moment he should make this presentation, and there had been no opportunity to alter this prearranged programme. So the great chief hesitated, held out the fatal belt, and then made a motion as though to withdraw it. Gladwyn extended his hand. As he did so, there came a rattling clash of arms from a passageway at the lower end of the hall and a deafening din of drums.

Pontiac started, dropped the belt of wampum, thrust a hand within his blanket, as though to draw a weapon, reconsidered, folded his arms, and stood motionless. In an instant all was again silent, and Gladwyn rose to address the council as though nothing out of the ordinary had happened.

He told the Indians that he would consider their grievances, and would do all that lay in his power to afford them protection, so long as they deserved it. At the same time he threatened them with a terrible punishment should they undertake to remedy their wrongs by any act of aggression against the whites. Then he dismissed the council, and the crestfallen warriors were allowed to leave the fort. Before departing, Pontiac notified the English commander that he should come again in a few days for another talk; but Gladwyn only turned contemptuously away, without deigning a reply.

Two days later the common behind the fort was again thronged with Indians, representing four tribes, and from out the throng Pontiac again approached the gate. It was barred against him, and when he demanded admittance, Gladwyn himself replied, ordering him to begone, as neither he nor his rabble would again be received.

Furious with rage, the chief strode away, and ordered his warriors to withdraw beyond gunshot, but to see that no Englishman was allowed to leave the fort. Then launching a canoe he crossed the river to his own village, which he ordered to be removed to the western bank.

While he was thus occupied, his infuriated followers were engaged in the murder and scalping of two English families who dwelt beyond reach of the fort. That night the inmates of Detroit, armed and sleepless, listened with heavy hearts to the doleful sounds of the scalp dance, mingled with the exulting yells of the war dance, and while prepared to sell their lives as dearly as possible, wondered how long their frail defences would withstand the fierce onset which they momentarily expected would be made against them.

Daylight found many of them, exhausted by the night's vigil, dozing at their posts. Suddenly the blood-curdling war-whoop arose from all sides at once, a rattling volley of rifle-shots pattered against the palisades, and a swarm of yelling, naked figures leaped from the surrounding obscurity. It seemed as though the impetuous assault must succeed from mere force of numbers, for the Indians were counted by hundreds, while the whites were but a handful.

CHAPTER XI
MAJOR HESTER IS TAKEN PRISONER

In spite of the apparent fury of the attack, and the expectation of the garrison that a fierce assault was about to be made on their slender defences, nothing of the kind was contemplated by the Indians. They were not trained to that form of warfare, and when they found that Gladwyn was not frightened into a surrender by noise and an exhibition of force, they contented themselves with maintaining a vigorous fire from behind barns, fences, bushes, slight ridges of earth, or any object of sufficient size to shelter them from the steady return fire of the soldiers. One cluster of buildings, within half-gunshot of the fort, sheltered a large body of Indians, who from this point of vantage directed a particularly galling fire at the loop-holes in the palisades. By it several of the defenders were wounded, until finally a cannon was brought to bear upon the hornet's nest, and a quantity of red-hot spikes were thrust into its muzzle. A minute after its discharge flames burst from the buildings, and the savages who had occupied them were in precipitate flight, followed by jeering shouts and a parting volley from the soldiers.

For six hours was this travesty of battle maintained. Then the Indian fire slackened, and finally ceased altogether. Believing the affair to be merely a temporary outbreak of a few hot-headed savages, that must quickly blow over, Gladwyn took advantage of this lull in the storm to send out two Canadians under a flag of truce to investigate the cause of dissatisfaction. At the same time he proposed, while negotiations were in progress, to secure a supply of provisions with which to stand a siege.

A gate being opened for the departure of the ambassadors, most of the Canadian inhabitants of the fort seized the opportunity to leave it, saying that they could not bear to remain and witness the approaching slaughter of their English friends.

In a short time Gladwyn's messengers returned, saying that Pontiac was willing to arrange terms, but would only do so with Major Hester, and had expressed a strong desire for a visit from that officer.

"Go back and tell him I will see him and his whole cowardly crew hanged, before I will intrust the life of a single Englishman to his treachery!" exclaimed the commander, angrily.

"Hold, Gladwyn!" protested Major Hester. "It is better that one life should be risked than that all should be endangered. Nor do I think I should be in any serious peril. I have always got along with the redskins, and have thus far found Pontiac reasonable."

"I forgot. He did present the calumet to you," replied the other, with a meaning intonation.

"Do you dare insinuate--?" began Major Hester, with a dangerous glitter in his eye.

"No, Hester. No, I do not. I am ashamed of myself and humbly apologize!" cried Gladwyn. "If you insist upon placing yourself within the power of yonder savages, I shall know that you do so from the loftiest sense of duty, with a full knowledge that you jeopardize your life, and with a courage that I fear I for one could not exhibit."

"Thank you, Gladwyn. That was said manfully and like a true soldier. I shall accept this mission because it is plainly in the line of my duty to do so. If I never return from it, I charge you to carry a father's blessing to my children."

The fine old soldier, in full uniform, was accompanied to the gateway by all the officers of the post. There every one shook hands with him, bidding him at once God-speed and farewell, while the soldiers lined the ramparts, and as he emerged from the gates saluted him with a rousing British cheer.

The major was escorted by the two aged Canadians who had been sent out in the first place, and the little party had not covered more than half the ground between the fort and Parent's creek, beyond which lay the Ottawa village, ere they were met by another Canadian running and breathless. He implored them to turn back, saying that he had just been through the Indian village and was convinced by what he saw and heard that no Englishman could set foot within its limits and live. But Major Hester steadfastly refused to retreat, and insisted on fulfilling his mission.

At length they crossed the creek, mounted the ridge beyond, and saw outspread on its further slope the most extensive Indian village ever known to that region. The moment the hated English uniform was seen by the inmates of the many lodges, they swarmed about the ambassadors by hundreds, the men with scowling brows, the squaws and children snatching up sticks, stones, and clubs as they ran. For a moment the stout heart of the old soldier quailed, for he imagined he was to be subjected to the terrible ordeal of the gantlet.

At the same time not a trace of emotion appeared on his face, as calmly folding his arms he stepped a pace or two in front of his shrinking companions and boldly confronted the throng of yelling savages. In another moment they would have overwhelmed him. Suddenly the stately form of Pontiac appeared among the rabble, and at the sound of his imperious voice they slunk aside like whipped curs. Instantly the tumult was allayed. In the silence that followed, the great chief greeted the British officer with a grave courtesy, shook his hand, and conducted him into the village.

The Ottawa encampment was a confused assemblage of tall, cone-shaped lodges, built of slender poles supporting great sheets of bark or overlapping folds of fine matting so closely woven from rushes as to be thoroughly rain-proof. Scores of graceful birch canoes, such as the northern tribes excel in making, were drawn up on the river bank; paddles and spears leaned against the lodges, smoke-blackened kettles and other rude cooking-utensils were scattered about the smouldering fires, and a throng of wolfish-looking dogs added their discordant baying to the clamor of children.

At the council lodge, which was conspicuous from its size, Major Hester was offered a seat on one of a circle of mats. As he took it, the other mats, as well as every inch of standing-room, were immediately occupied by a throng of warriors, while the entrance was crowded by many others, all eager to catch a glimpse of the Englishman.

After the tedious ceremony of smoking the peace pipe was concluded, Pontiac delivered a short address of welcome, to which the major responded. He demanded to know the cause of the morning's outbreak, and assured the Indians that their just grievances should be remedied, provided they gave up for punishment all who had been implicated in the murders of the previous day.

The major resumed his seat upon the conclusion of his remarks, amid a profound silence that lasted for many minutes. Finally, determined to learn the worst without further delay, he again rose and said, that having no answer to his questions, he would now return to the fort and report to the white chief that his red brothers desired not peace, but war.

Upon this Pontiac signed to him to resume his seat, and turning to the two Canadians, said:--

"Go to the fort and tell Major Gladwyn that the white-haired chief will sleep among the lodges of his red brothers. Tell him that the hatchet dug up this day will not be buried so long as an Englishman remains in the land of the Algonquins. Tell him that every fort from the Thunder of Waters to the Great River has this day been cut off, so that no aid may come to him. Tell him that the soldiers of the French king are already hastening to fight beside their red brothers. Tell him that he may go now and go in peace; but if he tarries beyond the setting of another sun, the wolves of the forest shall feast on the bodies of his red-coated soldiers, while their scalps shall dry in Ottawa lodges. Go, for Pontiac has spoken."

With trembling alacrity the Canadians obeyed the mandate, and with their departure Major Hester realized that he was indeed a prisoner in the hands of a relentless foe. While wondering as to his ultimate fate, he was conducted by Pontiac to a comfortable French frame-house standing just beyond the Indian village, and informed that this was to be his lodging.

"Here," said Pontiac, "shall my brother dwell in safety; but let him not set foot outside. My young men are angry, and their guns are quick to shoot. Even in the dark their eyes are opened wide by the sight of an English scalp."

"I suppose that as your prisoner I must submit to your orders," replied Major Hester, "though why you don't put an end to this farce and kill me at once I fail to comprehend."

"Did the white-haired chief kill me when I slept in the house of the two trees?" demanded Pontiac.

"When did you ever sleep in Tawtry House? Certainly you never did with my knowledge and consent."

"Many years have passed, and there has been much fighting since that time; but surely my brother has not forgotten Songa the Ottawa?"

"No. I remember him well; but what has he to do with this present affair?"

"I," replied the chief, drawing himself proudly up to his full height, "am Pontiac; but I was Songa; and as Major Hester saved the life of Songa, so Pontiac saves the life of Major Hester, by detaining him in this place while the English fort is wiped from the face of the earth and all within it are put to death."

CHAPTER XII
DONALD AT JOHNSON CASTLE

Some two weeks after the events just narrated, a youth, tanned to the swarthiness of an Indian, whose hair was long and unkempt, and whose well-worn suit of buckskin evidenced hard and prolonged travel, paced impatiently to and fro in the anteroom of Sir William's private office at Johnson Castle. Although his moccasined feet made no sound on the uncarpeted floor, his movements seemed to annoy the elder of two officers who, in handsome uniforms, occupied a window-seat at one side of the room, and were evidently waiting for somebody or something as patiently as their natures would permit.

"Confound the fellow!" he exclaimed. "Why can't he sit still and possess his soul in patience, like the rest of us, instead of tramping up and down like the wild beast he looks?"

"He doesn't make much noise about it," laughed the other.

"No, hang him! I wish he did. That cat-like tread of his is unendurable."

"He looks anxious, and doubtless has urgent business with Sir William that suffers from delay."

"Nonsense, Christie! you are too good natured. His business probably concerns payment for some game he has brought in for sale; for I take it he is one of these American hunters we have heard so much of lately. Whatever it is, it certainly can't compare in urgency with ours, and yet we have sat here like lambs for nearly an hour, while he has waited barely half that time. By the great horn spoon! If his serene highness does not admit us to his presence in a few minutes more, I shall beard him in his den, and demand audience in the name of the king. It is simply maddening to think of Cuyler carrying the Rothsay party farther and farther away with each minute, and having the beauty all to himself. Of course you don't care, since it was decided that they travel by the north shore of the lake, while, as I understand it, your beastly post lies somewhere on the south shore. With me, though, it is different. My destination being the same as hers, I naturally expected to be her travelling companion and enjoy a fair share of her charming society. Now what, with dancing attendance for a week on Sir Jeffry, and this abominable delay, I fear my chances of overtaking the expedition are very slim. By the way, I heard somewhere that the little Rothsay's name is not Rothsay, after all. Do you know if that is true, and if so, what her name really is?"

"I believe it is Hester,--Edith Hester," answered the young officer, who was addressed as Christie.

"I wonder how you always manage to find out such things?" remarked the other, reflectively. "By Jove!" he added, "Hester is the name of that major duffer whose message to Sir Jeffry caused my delay; I wonder if they can be relations?"

"," warned Christie, with a significant glance toward the third occupant of the room, who had paused in his restless walk and was regarding them intently.

Before the elder man could reply, he stepped, to where they were sitting and said quietly to the young officer who had just spoken:--

"Pardon my presumption in thus addressing a stranger, sir, but I feel it my duty to remind you that the word may receive several interpretations. In one sense, it cannot be exchanged between gentlemen without creating ill feelings. Its use by Terence--"

Ere the sentence could be completed, and while the bewildered officers were gazing at this backwoods expounder of the classics much as they might have regarded an apparition, a door was flung open, and Sir William Johnson appeared with an anxious expression on his ruddy and usually jolly face.

"Ah, general," exclaimed the officer who had just declared his intention of bearding the general in his den, "we had begun to think--"

"Glad you had, sir! Glad you had! Pray keep it up for a few minutes longer while I confer with this gentleman. His business is of such a nature as to take precedence of all other. Hester, my dear fellow, step this way."

"Rather a go! eh, Bullen?" remarked Ensign Christie, as the two men stared blankly at the door just closed in their faces.

"Well! By Jove!" gasped the other. "If His Majesty's officers were never snubbed before, two of them have been given a jolly big dose of it this time. All on account of that leather-jerkined young savage, too. I swear I'll have my man insult him and give him a thrashing at the first opportunity."

"You seem to forget," suggested Christie, gravely, "that your 'young savage' was discoursing most learnedly upon the idiosyncrasies of the Latin tongue when Sir William interrupted and called him 'my dear fellow.'"

"By Jove! you are right!" cried Bullen. "Possibly he is a gentleman in disguise,--best disguise I ever saw,--and in that case I can call him out. You'll act for me, old man, of course?"

"Certainly," laughed Christie; "but you lose sight of the fact that, as the challenged party, he will have the choice of weapons. Suppose he should select hunting-rifles at one hundred paces?"

"Horrible!" exclaimed Bullen. "I say, though, he couldn't do that and be a gentleman at the same time. Oh dear, no! Unless he names swords or pistols,--the only gentlemanly weapons,--I shall be compelled to withdraw in favor of Tummas."

"There is another point to be considered," continued Christie, who, tall, handsome, and easy-going, delighted in chaffing his pompous and peppery companion, whose abbreviated stature had only gained admittance to the service through high heels and a powerful influence. "Did you notice that Sir William addressed your 'young savage' as Hester?"

"Oh, by Jove! Yes; now that you mention it," cried the other, with an accent of despair. "And you said her name was Hester, too. The adorable little Rothsay to whom I had even proposed to propose. If this is a sample of her family though! But, of course, it can't be. It would be too incredible. She is an angel; while he--well, he isn't, and therefore cannot be even a remote connection."

Just here the door was again opened, and Sir William, followed by the subject of their conversation, re-entered the room.

"Well, general!" began the ever-impatient Bullen. "I trust you are not going to detain us here much longer. It is of the utmost importance that I should reach Detroit as speedily as possible."

"Ah, yes," replied the general, who knew that Paymaster Bullen had obtained his present detail solely for the sake of furthering certain schemes of his own. "I understand that you are going to investigate the unaccountable disappearance of a red blanket and a plug of tobacco from the quartermaster's stores at Detroit."

"Not only that, Sir William, but I am to make a very thorough inquiry into the unaccounted-for disappearance of a great many red blankets, and a great many plugs of tobacco, and a great many other things as well," answered the little paymaster, warmly.

"Very well, sir," replied the general. "If that is the sole object of your journey, you need not go beyond this room to acquire all necessary information. I can tell you what became of the goods in question, and who is responsible for their disappearance. I am indirectly; though my very dear friend, Major Graham Hester, recently in command at Detroit, acting by my advice, was the agent through whom they were distributed in the shape of presents to the warlike western tribes. By this means, and through his most excellent judgment in Indian affairs, Major Hester has succeeded in averting, until now, a bloody war, which has been imminent at any time during the last three years. Now, owing to a parsimony that withholds those few paltry dollars' worth of presents and the criminal stupidity of some of our newly arrived officers, we are on the eve of the most serious native outbreak this country has ever witnessed. As it is under the leadership of Pontiac, a man who I honestly believe would be unexcelled among the commanders of the world had he the advantages of education and environment, it is certain to prove a very formidable affair."

"Do I understand you, sir, that this outbreak has already taken place?" demanded Ensign Christie, who had just been assigned to his first independent command,--that of Presque Isle.

"My private despatches from Major Hester give me every reason for that belief," was the answer; "though Gladwyn does not mention it. Ensign Hester, who brings these despatches, confirms his father's warning. He, moreover, informs me that the Senecas have joined the conspiracy, he and his companion having had a narrow escape from a west-bound party of that tribe. As it was, the Indians stole their canoe, leaving them to make their way on foot for over two hundred miles through the forest to this place. Thus, too, they missed meeting with Cuyler's command, which they were charged to warn of the threatened danger."

"May I ask if this is Ensign Hester?" inquired Christie, turning with an engaging smile toward the leather-clad young stranger.

"Bless my soul! Yes. Haven't you met him? Ensign Christie and Paymaster Bullen, permit me to present Ensign Donald Hester of the 60th, son of my dear friend the major, and brother of the very prettiest girl I know. By the way, lad, I believe I haven't told you the worst bit of news yet. It is that your giddy sister has persuaded Madam Rothsay to take her to Detroit as a delightful surprise for your father. They accompany Cuyler's expedition by especial permission of the general, who of course never doubted that in a time of profound peace the journey might be made in safety. And Cuyler, who did not expect to leave before this time, has already been gone a week, his movements having been greatly hastened, I fancy, by impetuous Miss Edith."

"I had already heard something of this," answered Donald, with a meaning glance at the two officers, "and had made up my mind to start at once on Cuyler's trail, with a view to overtaking and--please God--warning him in time."

"So be it, lad. Much as I hate to have you go without first taking a spell of rest, it is so clearly the thing to do that I cannot but bid you God-speed," exclaimed Sir William.

"Mr. Hester," said Christie, "I beg you will forgive and forget the rudeness of which I was guilty a few minutes since. I ought to have recognized a gentleman at sight under any conditions, and am ashamed to confess that for the moment I failed to do so."

"It is not at all to be wondered at, Mr. Christie," answered Donald, grasping the other's extended hand, "and as I have already forgotten the incident, I can find nothing to forgive."

"And will you allow me, as a great favor, to accompany you on this return trip so far as our ways lie together?"

"Gladly, though I warn you that I shall travel fast and hard."

"I will risk it," laughed Christie, "and to a novice in woodcraft like myself I know that such companionship as yours will prove invaluable."

"Well, hang it all, Christie! If you are going, I don't see why I shouldn't go too," sputtered Bullen, and while Donald would gladly have dispensed with the paymaster's company, he could not well frame an excuse for so doing.

CHAPTER XIII
PAYMASTER BULLEN AND HIS WONDERFUL TUB

Though Donald had not the art to rid himself of an undesirable travelling-companion, Fate, in the shape of a tin bath-tub, interposed in his behalf. This tub was the little paymaster's pride and delight, for in a measure it was his own invention. Having had it constructed in England especially for use in America, he had become so enamored of it that by this time he would sooner have parted with any other possession. It was a round affair, about three feet in diameter, had a high back, was painted green on the outside and white within. Here its resemblance to ordinary bath-tubs ended, and its individuality became apparent. To begin with, it was built with double sides about three inches apart, and the space thus formed was divided by metallic partitions into many compartments, of different sizes, all of which were provided with close-fitting, water-tight lids. These could only be opened by the pressing of a cleverly concealed spring. Not only did this hollow and cellular construction give great buoyancy to the tub, adapting it for use as a life preserver, but the compartments afforded safe storage room for a number of toilet articles, such as are generally difficult to obtain in the wilderness. For the present trip, the paymaster had laid in a liberal supply of scented soap, tooth powder, perfumery, pomades, cosmetics, brushes, shaving-utensils, and innumerable other adjuncts of a dandy's dressing-table; for in spite of his tendency toward stoutness and his uncertain age, Paymaster Bullen was emphatically a dandy, with an ambition to be considered a beau.

Equally interesting with the body of this unique tub was its high back. At the touch of a spring a small panel on the inside slid to one side, disclosing a mirror. By the pressing of two other springs, one on each side, the entire back could be tilted to the angle most comfortable for repose, if one happened to be sitting in the body of the tub. The back was covered, as though for protection, by a sheet of canvas. This could be drawn up, half of it pulled forward over the top, like a hood or canopy. Held in this position by an ingenious arrangement of umbrella ribs, it formed a protection against sun or rain. On the whole, Paymaster Bullen's bathtub was a remarkable institution, and one to which he was so attached that he would on no account undertake a journey on which it might not accompany him.

"How could I take my regular morning bath without it? or how could I transport the necessities of my toilet so safely and conveniently in any other way?" were to him unanswerable arguments in its favor.

It was useless to reply that a tub might be dispensed with in a country abounding in streams and lakes, or that the niceties of the toilet were not always considered in the wilderness.

He would answer, that while the crude bathing facilities afforded by nature might suffice for the primitive requirements of the untutored savage, a tub was a necessity to which he, as a refined product of civilization, had always been accustomed, and did not propose to forego. Also that to the toilet of an officer and a gentleman certain well-recognized adjuncts were as indispensable in the wilderness as in the town.

He spent so much of his leisure sitting or reclining in his beloved tub, gloating over its many admirable points and reflecting upon its possibilities, that his brother officers rarely spoke of him by any other name than that of "Diogenes."

Donald Hester of course knew nothing of the wonderful tub, nor of another whim of the paymaster's, which was that an officer should never appear in public save in uniform. Consequently, when the little man approached the canoe landing, resplendent in scarlet and gold, and followed by his valet staggering beneath the weight of the tub, Donald turned to Ensign Christie for an explanation of the phenomenon, while the latter expressed his feelings by a prolonged whistle. Two canoes and several Indian canoemen had been provided by Sir William for the transportation of the party. Christie had exchanged his uniform for a flannel shirt, gray breeches, leggings, and moccasins, and except for Mr. Bullen's presence everything was in readiness for departure.

"Hello, Bullen! you surely do not intend to traverse the wilderness in full fig.?" cried Sir William, who had come down to speed his guests. "You seem to forget that much of your way may traverse the country of an enemy, for whose rifles your gorgeousness would offer a bright and shining mark."

"Nor to take your man with you. Of course, Bullen, you don't intend to do that?" remonstrated Christie.

"If that is your luggage, Mr. Bullen," added Donald, indicating the tub with a gesture, "I'm afraid it must be left behind, or we shall never overtake Cuyler."

"Sir William," retorted the paymaster with all the dignity he could assume, "I always travel in uniform. Being honored with the wearing of His Majesty's livery, I cannot conceive why it should not be displayed before his enemies as well as to his friends.--Mr. Christie: never having journeyed without an attendant, I do not now propose to attempt the experiment.--Mr. Hester: I have very grave duties to perform at Detroit, and feel it to be of importance to produce an impression there from the very first. Therefore I find it necessary to take with me on this journey certain articles that a less conscientious person might possibly leave behind."

"But, sir, this is a matter of life or death, and we dare not allow anything to delay us," said Donald, earnestly.

"Very well, sir, proceed on your journey without regard to me, and I will follow in such fashion as seems to me best. It may prove that I shall not be so very far behind when your destination is reached. At any rate, I assure you that I am thoroughly capable of conducting my own movements."

"Oh come, Bullen! Act sensibly, and leave all useless lumber behind," urged Ensign Christie.

"Mr. Christie, I always act sensibly, according to my own definition of the word, and I absolutely refuse to leave my tub behind," replied the paymaster, in a frigid tone.

"Gentlemen, I cannot delay another moment," cried Donald, who was in a fever of impatience. "With your permission, Sir William, Mr. Christie and I will take the smaller of these canoes, leaving the other, with all the Indians, for Mr. Bullen's service."

"Go ahead, my boy; you are right. Good-bye, and God bless you!" answered the general, heartily. So in another minute Donald and his newly acquired friend had set forth on their long journey. Both wielded paddles, for Ensign Christie had already seen enough of service in America to have gained a fair degree of skill in canoeing.

For hours these two paddled, poled, and tracked their way against the swift current of the Mohawk, until utter darkness barred their further progress. Then they made a blind landing, groped about for a few sticks, kindled a small fire over which to make a pot of tea, and flung themselves down for a few hours of sleep on the bare ground. The next morning they were up, had eaten breakfast, and were off by daybreak. Before dark of that day they had crossed the portage, and were floating with the current of Wood creek. Only pausing at the blockhouse to deliver a despatch from Sir William, they crossed Oneida lake in darkness, and spent the night at Fort Brewerton. The following night found them well past Oswego and camped on the shore of Lake Ontario.

In all this ceaseless labor, Ensign Christie proved of the greatest assistance, and heartily commended himself to his companion by his unflagging cheerfulness. He was always ready to jump overboard, at the first intimation that such a move was necessary, to use a push-pole or paddle, gather wood, or to perform any service that lay within his power. Often, as the young men made their swift way along the south shore of the great lake, did they talk of Paymaster Bullen and wonder what had become of him. Donald was inclined to believe that he had either returned to New York, or still remained where they had left him; but Christie only smiled, and said Bullen was such a queer fish that there was no predicting what he might or might not do.

On the evening of the third day after leaving Oswego, shortly before sunset, and aided by a strong breeze blowing up the lake, they ran alongside the canoe landing at Fort Niagara. Major Wilkins, the commandant, and several of his officers met them as they stepped from their craft, when a rapid exchange of introductions and news was at once begun.

Suddenly some one exclaimed, "What boat is that following so close after you?" and, looking in the direction indicated, all saw a small craft driven at a high rate of speed by both sail and paddle, rapidly approaching the landing.

No one could imagine who it was, but many conjectures were hazarded, until the canoe drew near enough for its occupants to be distinguished. Then Ensign

Christie shouted with unfeigned amazement:

"By Jove! It's old Bullen himself!"

CHAPTER XIV
A WHITE MEDICINE MAN

Ensign Christie was right in his conjecture, for the new arrival was Paymaster Bullen. His canoe, which he had requisitioned at Oswego, was of the largest size, and in addition to six Indian paddlers was provided with a square sail, for use before fair winds. In the middle of this craft, seated in his beloved tub as on a throne, appeared the doughty paymaster, in full uniform. This included a cocked hat, carefully powdered wig, laced coat, sword, perfectly fitting breeches, white silk stockings, and high-heeled pumps, surmounted by large silver buckles. As the big canoe dashed up to the beach, it was noticed that its native crew dropped their paddles and flung themselves down as though utterly exhausted. With a contemptuous glance at them, the little paymaster stepped carefully ashore, and addressing the commander of the post, who advanced to meet him, said:--

"Major Wilkins, I believe. My name is Bullen,--Leonidas Bullen,--and I hold a requisition upon you signed by Sir Jeffry Amherst, for a boat and crew to carry me with all speed to Detroit, on the king's business. You will also please furnish the natives who have brought me to this point with goods, according to the subjoined list. Take their receipt for same and permit them to return to Oswego. That is all, sir, and I should be pleased to proceed with the least possible delay."

"I am at your service, paymaster," replied Major Wilkins, courteously, as he glanced over the papers just handed to him, "and you shall be forwarded with all speed. But you will surely spend the night with us. We--"

"Couldn't think of it, my dear sir! couldn't think of it for a moment, delighted as I should be to do so," interrupted the new arrival. "You see, my mission is of such urgency. Then, too, I am desirous of overtaking my young friends Christie and Hester before--By Jove! there they are now! What are you chaps doing here? I thought you were in a hurry to get on."

"Oh, Bullen! how could you have imagined such a thing?" asked Christie, gravely, as he shook hands with his recent travelling-companion. "We were in haste to leave Johnson Castle, to be sure, but since then--why, my dear fellow, we have simply loafed, in the hope that you would overtake us, and having waited here as long as we dared, were just about to retrace our course in search of you."

"Yes indeed," added Donald, readily taking the cue from his friend; "we have been so distressed at your non-appearance that we really could not have waited any longer. Then, too, you know one can so easily exhaust the resources of a place like this in twenty-four hours."

"Twenty-four hours!" gasped Bullen. "Have you chaps really been here twenty-four hours?"

"More or less," assented Christie, cheerfully. "But where have you been lingering all this time? We thought you must have returned to New York. Oh, I remember! There were attractions at Oswego. Eh, Bullen! you fickle dog, you?"

"Confound you! I haven't lingered," sputtered the little paymaster, whose face was rapidly assuming an apoplectic hue.

"Indeed, you have not, paymaster," broke in Major Wilkins, coming to his rescue, "for, from the Oswego date on this letter, I see you have broken the record and made the fastest time ever known between here and there. These chaps only got in a few minutes ahead of you, and I'll warrant you gave them at least a day's start. How did you manage it?"

"Oh, you villains!" cried the mollified paymaster, shaking his fist at the laughing subalterns. "Never mind, I'll get even with you!" Then, to the major, he replied: "I confess I was somewhat impatient to get here, and so I allowed my crew to work nights as well as in the daytime. In that way we came through without a stop, save such as were necessary for the cooking of our meals."

"But I never heard of such a thing!" exclaimed the astonished major. "It is all I can do to keep Indian crews at work from sunrise to within an hour of sunset, and they always insist on being in camp before dark. What inducements did you offer them?"

"None at all," replied the paymaster, calmly. "I just let them have their own way. They chose to do it. I expect they saw I was in a hurry and wanted to oblige me."

This was all the information on the subject that could be gleaned from the paymaster at that time; but as he was now easily persuaded to join Donald and Christie in remaining at the post over night, the officers still entertained hopes of extracting his secret. In this they finally succeeded; for that evening, after the little man had been mellowed by a capital dinner, he consented to account for the remarkable influence he had gained over the savages.

"It is all very simple, gentlemen," he said, "and is merely one of the minor triumphs of knowledge over ignorance. On my journey from Johnson Castle to the lake I had not made very good time, and saw that only by heroic measures could I hope to overtake my volatile young friends here, before they passed this point. At Oswego I procured a larger craft and a fresh crew. From the outset I saw that these fellows regarded my innocent tub with a certain degree of suspicion, and soon gave them to understand, through one of their number who could speak some English, that it held a powerful fire-demon. He was quite capable, I declared, of destroying every Indian on the continent, and would be at liberty to do so, if he was not thrown into the great thunder waters--your cataract, you understand--on, or before, the first day of the new moon, which I calculated would be visible tomorrow evening. I assured them that his power was much less on water than on land, for which reason I could not allow his prison house--alias my bath-tub--to be carried ashore short of this place. With all this, I gave them to understand that I was something of a fire-king myself, for which reason I had been intrusted with this important mission."

"But I don't see how you persuaded the beggars to believe in such rot," objected Christie.

"Ah, my dear boy! Genius can find ways and means for persuading Faith to any belief. These simple children of nature have implicit faith in the supernatural. As for genius--well, some persons possess it, while others do not, and modesty forbids my making invidious comparisons. Seeing by their incredulous smiles that the several members of my crew were inclined to doubt my statements, and were determined to pass the first night on shore as usual, I began to impersonate the Fire King as soon as we made a landing. To begin with, I ordered my man to bring me a cup of boiling water, as I was thirsty. Being a well-trained beggar, he obeyed without betraying any surprise. Pretending to taste it, and declaring that it was too cold, I threw it, cup and all, angrily away. Then I dipped a glass of water from the lake, announcing at the same time that by the power of my magic I could make it boil more furiously than any fire that ever burned."

"A bold statement. By Jove!" exclaimed one of the officers, who were following this narration with closest attention; "but did you make it good?"

"Certainly," replied the paymaster, gravely. "I not only made that water boil furiously within two seconds, but immediately drank it. You see I happened to have in a compartment of my tub an effervescing powder, which I find a wholesome aperient. Making a magic pass with my hand, I dropped a small quantity of this into the glass undetected. The effect was instantaneous, and as the liquid boiled above the rim of the glass so that all could see it, I tossed it off, remarking casually to Tummas as I did so, that when I called for boiling water I meant water that was actually boiling, and not merely warm."

"Well, by Jove!" was heard in admiring accents from various corners of the mess table.

"My guileless savages were evidently impressed, but not yet inclined to move," continued the little paymaster, without noticing the interruption, "so I concluded to arouse them by another and more startling exhibition of my powers. Having hinted that the little fire devils of the forest, which I fancy every savage has seen, at one time or another, peering at him from rotten tree trunks, logs, or stumps, might be attracted by the proximity of the great Fire Demon, I strolled off a short distance, as though to search for them. From my tub I had previously taken an old scratch wig and a small box of phosphorus paste, for which I have a certain use. It was by this time quite dark. With my paste I drew the rude outline of a face on a bit of bark, that I stood at the base of a tree. Then rubbing some of the stuff on my old wig, and clapping it on my head, I ran back to camp, shouting that I had found one, and that he had attempted to seize me by the hair. The savages, who had been lying down, sprang to their feet, and uttered yells of terror at sight of my blazing head. 'There he is now!' I shouted, pointing back to the phosphorescent face. 'Shoot him quick, or he will catch us!'

"Without waiting for them to get their guns from the canoe, I picked up a stone and let it drive with all my might. There was a loud explosion, the dreadful face disappeared, and at the same moment we all broke for the canoe, which we shoved off in a hurry. As we pulled out from the shore I nearly paralyzed my crew by tearing off the old wig--my scalp, as they thought--and flinging it into the water, where we could distinguish its phosphorescent glow for some minutes. After that experience, my slightest wish was law to those savages, nor could anything have tempted them to pass a night on shore in company with the caged Fire Demon. They are now confident that he is to be thrown into the thunder waters to-morrow, and so I want them started back toward Oswego before that illusion is dispelled. Otherwise my influence over future crews may be weakened. Now, gentlemen, you have my simple receipt for rapid travelling in the wilderness."

"But, Bullen! How about the explosion of that bit of rock?" inquired several voices at once.

"Simplicity itself. It was replaced in my hand, as I picked it up, by a ball of clay, previously prepared for the occasion. It contained a pinch of fulminate and a few bits of gravel."

"Well, paymaster, I must confess that your ingenuity is most creditable!" commented Major Wilkins. "I foresee that we must hasten your departure in the morning; for if your fame as Fire King and that of the demon caged in your tub should precede you to the head of the river, I should never be able to secure a crew to take you to Detroit. Therefore, gentlemen, in anticipation of early rising, I give you a farewell toast: Our guest the Fire King; may he long continue a bright and shining ornament to His Majesty's service."

This toast was drunk with a hearty cheer; the little paymaster bowed his acknowledgments, and with much laughter the merry party broke up for the night.

CHAPTER XV
DONALD AND CHRISTIE CEMENT A FRIENDSHIP

The ready wit and fertility of resource, shown by Paymaster Bullen on the speedy journey he had just accomplished, gave Donald such a different impression of the man, from that conceived at their first meeting, that he was now quite willing to accept him as a travelling companion. This he was the more ready to do, as from the upper end of the Niagara river he must part company with Christie, whose course would be along the south shore of the lake, while, to follow Cuyler's expedition, Donald and the paymaster must skirt the northern shore. Consequently it was arranged that while Christie should continue his journey in a bateau that was about to carry several recruits to Presque Isle, the others, including "Tummas," should be provided with a large canoe and a crew of four Seneca Indians. Donald's belief that the Senecas were about to go on the war-path, if indeed they had not already done so, was not shared by Major Wilkins, who declared it could not possibly be, as he was in constant communication with prominent members of that tribe, and had discovered no indication of ill-feeling toward the whites. The major also ridiculed the idea that any of the western Indians would dare wage war against the English, now that they could no longer hope for French assistance.

"Much as I respect your father's judgment in such matters, my dear boy," he said to Donald, as they parted early on the following morning, "I am certain that in the present case he must be mistaken. If fear of an Indian outbreak is all that keeps him at Detroit, tell him from me that he may return east at once, bringing his pretty daughter, your charming sister, with him. Tell him, too, that we shall expect him to make a long visit at Fort Niagara . We are all longing for a further acquaintance with Miss Edith; for though I did succeed in detaining Cuyler two whole days solely on her account, her stay with us was far too short. Pray present my compliments to Madam Rothsay also, and tell her that we live only in the hope of her return.

"Yes, I mean it all, and a great deal more too," laughed the gallant major; "so speed your journey, that we may not die of despair. Good-bye and good luck to you, lad. Good-bye, Christie. Run over and call on us as often as your duties will permit. I fear you will find life at Presque Isle a deadly monotony. Farewell, paymaster. It is delightful to see the king's livery borne into the wilderness with such grace and dignity. I predict that you will make an impression at Detroit, upon whites as well as reds, and I will guarantee peace with the latter so long as you and your wonderful tub remain in the country. Bon voyage, gentlemen! Shove off!"

This last order was given to the crew of a light whale-boat, in which our travellers were already seated, and which was to convey them a few miles up the river to the lower end of the portage, where the town of Lewiston now stands. At that time it was the site of a fortified camp maintained for the protection of the men, pack-horses, and ox-teams employed in transporting freight over the rugged road between there and Fort Schlosser, a small post situated at the beginning of navigable waters above the falls.

Here the luggage of our party, including Bullen's tub, was transferred to an ox-wagon that was escorted by the paymaster on horseback, as he refused to lose sight of his belongings even for a short time. Scorning the horses proffered for their use, and delighting in the opportunity for stretching their legs, the two younger officers set briskly forth on foot, and were soon far in advance of the slow-moving wagon.

"I would that our journeyings beyond this point lay in the same direction, Hester," remarked Ensign Christie, when they found themselves alone. "Although we have not known each other long, I feel as though we were old friends, for I have rarely met a fellow to whom I have taken so great a liking in so short a time."

"Thank you, old man. For my part, I heartily reciprocate the feeling," replied Donald, "and I wish with all my heart that you were going to Detroit with me. Not only should I rejoice in your company, but I should like to have you meet my father and sister."

"I have already had the pleasure of meeting Miss Hester," rejoined Christie.

"You have!" exclaimed Donald; "when? where? why didn't you tell me before?"

"I met her at a ball given by General Amherst, the night before her departure from New York, and had the honor of dancing with her. That I have not mentioned the fact was because I feared to recall to you an unpleasant memory of a conversation between Bullen and myself, regarding her, that you must have overheard at Sir William's, that time, you know, when you so neatly floored my Latin."

"What an asinine thing that was, on my part," laughed Donald. "I only overheard a few bits of your conversation, and interrupted it in that stupid manner, for fear lest I should be tempted to act the eavesdropper. But tell me, since you have seen Edith so recently, is she so good looking as they say? I have not seen her for more than a year, you know."

"She is the most beautiful creature that ever I laid eyes on, as well as the sweetest and most charming," replied Christie, with such warmth that Donald eyed him curiously.

"It was the unanimous opinion of all the men who saw her that evening," continued Christie, flushing slightly beneath the other's searching gaze. "As for poor Bullen, he was so completely fascinated, that he had neither eyes nor speech for any one else, though there were dozens of charming girls present. But, I say, Hester! Saw you ever a more frightful place than this, or a more deadly situation for an ambuscade?"

Their road had, after its first sharp ascent from the river, followed the verge of those stupendous cliffs which rise sheer and bare on the eastern side of the mighty torrent that has channelled them. The young men had paused many times to gaze on the leaping surges and awful billows that raged in fury two hundred feet beneath them, or to listen, awe-struck, to the ceaseless thunder of falling waters, with which earth and air quivered. Now, within three miles of the cataract, they paused again on the brink of a lateral rent in the sheer wall of rock, so deep and black as to have won for itself the name of Devil's Hole. The road winding around the brink of this abyss was skirted on its further side by a steep and densely wooded slope. It was indeed a deadly place for an ambuscade, as several bodies of British troops subsequently discovered to their sorrow, and the young soldiers shuddered as they reflected upon its possibilities.

Suddenly, as they stood motionless and silent, Christie was amazed to have his companion spring from his side as though he had been shot, dart across the road, and disappear in the bushes beyond. There was a momentary sound of crackling sticks and swishing branches, and then all was still. Unable to account for this mysterious proceeding, and not knowing what action to take, Ensign Christie stood motionless, where he was left, for some minutes. Then Donald reappeared, walking down the road as calmly as though nothing extraordinary had happened, though breathing heavily from his recent exertions.

"The rascal was too quick for me," he said, as he rejoined his companion.

"What rascal? What do you mean?" asked the bewildered ensign.

"I don't know; wish I did. All I know is that it was an Indian, and that he was watching us. I noticed his tracks some distance back, and also noticed that just before we reached this point they turned abruptly into the underbrush. As we stood looking down that hole, I heard a twig snap, and knew he was close at hand. I thought I might surprise him, but, as I said, he was too quick for me, and I only caught a flying glimpse of him as he disappeared."

"Well, it seems curious," meditated Christie, "but I neither noticed any footprints nor heard a sound, save the thunder of yonder waters."

"It doesn't strike me so," replied Donald; "for if I had not been born and brought up in the woods, I should not be apt to notice such things either. As it is, I should feel very much ashamed not to have noticed them. Now, I think we had best wait here for the rest of the party. It is possible there may be mischief afoot. I wouldn't say anything to needlessly alarm the paymaster, though."

"All right," agreed Christie; "but what could be the chap's object in spying our movements?"

"It is hard to say; but I am satisfied that there is a general Indian war much nearer at hand than Major Wilkins is willing to admit, and in that case we must be prepared at any moment for all sorts of unexpected happenings. I only wish I was by my sister's side in one of Cuyler's boats, and could give the lieutenant warning of what to expect."

"So do I," assented Christie so heartily that the other looked at him quizzically, and he hastened to add, "I mean so do I wish you were there, though I trust you may be mistaken in your prophecy. In case there is any trouble, though, I hope I may reach my post before it breaks out."

"I hope you may, old man, with all my heart. At any rate, you want to keep both eyes and ears wide open every minute between here and there, and after you get there, too. Hello! Here comes Bullen!"

"By Jove! What a beastly place!" cried the little paymaster, as he peered into the dim depths of the Devil's Hole. "It actually makes one feel creepy, don't you know. Tummas, you rascal, gad up those snails of bulls and let us move on."

An hour later, as they came abreast of the stupendous cataract, whose mighty voice had throbbed in their ears all that morning, the younger men would gladly have lingered to gaze on its grandeur; but the paymaster complained that the volume of water was not nearly so great as he had been led to expect, and refused to waste any time in gazing on it.

"But surely, Bullen, you are going to drown the Fire Demon, and we want to see the last of the tub," expostulated Christie.

"You'll have to want then, and want till you're gray, and longer," retorted the little man. "So we might as well move on. Tummas, you idiot, gad up those bulls!"

CHAPTER XVI
QUICKEYE AND THE "ZEBRA"

The flotilla under command of Lieutenant Cuyler consisted of twenty bateaux, nineteen of which were heavily laden with recruits and supplies of ammunition, provisions, and goods for Fort Detroit. The other boat, which generally headed the fleet, was of lighter and more graceful construction than the others, and was reserved for the commander of the expedition. In it also travelled the two ladies, who were thus undertaking an adventurous journey into the far western wilderness. This much information concerning his sister's present surroundings Donald Hester gained at Fort Schlosser, from which place the flotilla had departed six days before his own arrival.

Six days! It was a long lead to overcome, and everything he dreaded might happen in that time. Still, he did not anticipate that the convoy would run into danger before it neared Detroit, which place it was not expected to reach in less than two weeks. If, therefore, he could overtake it within one week, or before it entered the Detroit river, all might yet be well. Having reached this conclusion, the young officer bustled about with such energy, that he had the satisfaction of getting his own party started from Fort Schlosser late that same afternoon, instead of waiting until the following morning, as had been at first planned.

Once under way, the active young fellow seized a paddle, and so aided the progress of the big canoe by his own efforts that ere darkness set in the river had been stemmed to its source, and the broad expanse of Lake Erie lay before them, still glimmering in the western glow. Not until they were well beyond the influence of the strong current setting toward the river, would he permit a landing to be made.

Donald had been perplexed from the start to find that there were five Indians in the canoe, instead of the four promised by Major Wilkins. He was also amazed to discover that none of them could speak English, for they all shook their heads with expressionless faces when he addressed them in that tongue. By using signs and the few Iroquois words that he could remember, he managed to make known his wishes; but, although these were obeyed, he imagined there was some mystery in the air, and became keenly watchful for its development.

From the very first he was suspicious of the fifth, or extra member, of the crew, who occupied the extreme stern of the canoe and acted as steersman. None of the Indians were very pleasant to look upon; but the face of this individual was so thickly covered with paint of many colors that its personality was concealed, as though by a mask. This paint being laid on in narrow stripes, Mr. Bullen was moved to call him the "Zebra," a name that seemed to please the fellow, and to which he readily answered.

That night the white men slept beneath the canoe, which was turned half over, with its upper gunwale resting on a couple of short, but stout, forked sticks; and, acting upon Donald's insistent advice, they kept watch by turn, two hours at a time, during the night. Even "Tummas" was so thoroughly impressed with a sense of responsibility, that his two hours of watchfulness were passed in a nervous tremble and with hardly a blink of his wide-open eyes. Donald stood the last watch, and at its conclusion he woke the Indians and ordered them to prepare breakfast.

Day was just breaking, and while two of the Indians attended to the fire the other three scattered through the woods in hopes of picking up some unwary bit of game. While they were thus engaged, Donald took a long refreshing swim in the cool waters of the lake. He did not arouse the paymaster until the hunters had returned, bringing a wild turkey and a few brace of pigeons, by which time breakfast was ready. Then, to his dismay, the little man insisted on having a bath in his tub, which proved a very tedious operation, on being shaved, and on performing so elaborate a toilet, that the sun was more than an hour high, and Donald was fuming with impatience, before they were ready to start.

All this time the Indians, who had swallowed their breakfast in silence, as well as with despatch, smoked their pipes and gazed with delighted wonder at the novel operations of "Tummas" and his master. As the several compartments of the tub yielded up their mysterious contents, the dusky spectators gave vent to ejaculations of amazement, and several times he of the striped face stepped forward for a closer inspection of the marvellous receptacle.

"I say, Bullen, this sort of thing will never do!" began Donald, when the paymaster was at length resplendent in his completed toilet, and they were once more under way. "We ought to have been off three hours ago. If we continue to waste time at this rate, there is no possible chance of overtaking Cuyler, and you know as well as I what that may mean to me."

"Yes, my dear fellow, I understand; but how can I help it? You can't, of course, expect a gentleman to go without his daily tub, and I assure you that in my desire to expedite our journey I haven't occupied more than half my usual time this morning."

Donald groaned. Then, with a happy thought, he inquired: "How would it do to take your bath in the evening, as soon as we make a landing, and while supper is being prepared?"

"It would be entirely contrary to custom," replied the other. "Still, it might be done for a short time, and for the sake of being accommodating I am willing to try it. I don't think you need fear, though, that we shall not pursue this journey with even more than ordinary speed, for I mean to appear before these rascals in my role of Fire King this very evening, and thereafter I fancy they will be only too anxious to push ahead, in order to be rid of me as quickly as possible."

"All right," replied Donald, "and I wish you success in it." Then he bent with redoubled energy over his paddle. In spite of his efforts, he was not satisfied with the progress made by the canoe. She appeared to drag. It did not seem as though the Indians were doing good work, and he spoke sharply to them several times in the course of the morning. He had a suspicion that the steersman often turned the flat of his paddle against the course of the canoe; but, as his back was turned, he could not be certain of this. What he did know for a surety was that, as they ran in toward the beach for a short midday halt, the Zebra, with unpardonable carelessness, allowed the frail craft to run against a sharp rock that cut a jagged gash in her birchen side. The next moment she was on the beach, so that no one got even a wetting; but a long delay ensued while a patch of bark was stitched over the rent and payed with pitch.

When at length all was again in readiness for a start, Donald calmly assumed the position of steersman in the stern, at the same time motioning the Zebra to take his place among the paddlers. The man hesitated a moment, seemed about to refuse, and then, with a second glance at the young officer's determined face, slowly obeyed the order. During the remainder of that afternoon the Indians labored at their paddles in silence, and with scowling brows. It was evident to Donald that a crisis of some kind was at hand. Even the paymaster noticed that an uncomfortable feeling prevailed in the boat, but he had implicit faith that his performance of that evening would set everything to rights.

"These fellows will be my abject slaves before I am done with them," he remarked cheerfully, and relying on their ignorance of English he explained fully what he proposed to do. Not only would he repeat the tricks that had already proved so successful, but he planned to complete the subjugation of these particular savages by causing certain green and blue flames to dance above their camp-fire. The whole was to conclude with a slight explosion, that should leave the scene in darkness, save for a weird phosphorescent light emanating from a face that would appear suspended in mid-air. This last effort, as the paymaster explained to Donald, he would produce by painting the face on a bit of bark that should be attached to a fish-line. One end of this should be tossed over the limb of a tree, and the affair should be jerked into position at the proper moment.

The projector of this entertainment was enthusiastic and confident. "Tummas," who was an interested listener to all that was said, chuckled audibly, as he reflected upon the dismay of the savages, and even Donald looked forward to the experiment with interest.

Alas! that such well-laid plans should be doomed to failure; but such was the lamentable fact. When, soon after landing, the paymaster called for boiling water, the Indians watched him swallow his effervescing mixture with unmoved faces. When he hurled a ball of clay, charged with fulminating powder, at a tree, missed his mark, and caused the missile to fall harmlessly in the water, they gazed at him pityingly. When, an hour later, he strolled over to their camp-fire and carelessly tossed what appeared to be a stone into it, they drew back a few paces, watched the play of colored flames that followed, with interest, and were not at all disturbed by the small explosion that took place a minute afterwards. To crown all, when their attention was attracted to a flaming face swinging in the darkness above their heads, the Zebra deliberately raised his gun and blew the bit of bark to atoms, with the point-blank discharge of a load of buckshot. Then the Indians calmly resumed their positions and their pipes, while the crestfallen author of this signal failure, unable to find words to express his feelings, sullenly retired to the canoe and rolled himself in a blanket.

The next morning, as Donald emerged from his plunge in the lake, he detected one of the Indians crouching beside the canoe, and evidently tampering with its bark covering. Naked as he was, the young fellow bounded to the spot and, ere the Indian was aware of his presence, knocked him sprawling with a single blow. Like a panther the savage sprang to his feet, and, knife in hand, rushed at his assailant. Suddenly he paused, his outstretched arm fell to his side, and he stood like one petrified, with his eyes fixed on Donald. Then, in excellent English, he said slowly:--

"Why did not Quickeye tell his red brother that he was of the Totem of the Bear and of the magic circle of the Metai?"

As he spoke, the Indian pointed to the rude device that, tattooed in blue lines, had ornamented Donald Hester's left arm, just below the shoulder, ever since he was an infant.

Instead of answering this question, the young man replied scornfully:--

"So you can speak English, can you, you red scoundrel? And you call me 'Quickeye' because I caught you peering from the bushes at the Devil's Hole, do you? Yes, I am quick-eyed enough to read every thought in your black heart. Do I not know that you came in the canoe with the white medicine man from Oswego? Do I not know that you listened outside the open window of the mess-room at Fort Niagara, while the white chiefs talked at night? Do I not know that you painted your face, with the thought that the white man was a fool and would no longer recognize you? Then you came in this canoe that you might make it go slow, like a swan whose wing is broken by the hunter. Do not I know all this as well as all the things you have done, and thought of doing? You are a fool! The Metai know everything. Bah! If I had not use for you, I would strike you dead. But I need your strength, and so long as you serve me truly you shall live. Go, and be ready to start ere the sun rises from yonder water."

With this the young man turned on his heel, while the humbled savage slunk away, cringing as though he had felt the lashing of whips. From that moment there was no further trouble, and the canoe of the white men was sped on its journey at a pace to satisfy even their impatience.

CHAPTER XVII
A BRAVE GIRL CAPTIVE

For two weeks after leaving the Niagara river Cuyler's boat brigade made its way slowly but steadily westward, along the northern, forest-covered shore of Lake Erie. Except for an occasional day of rain, when the expedition remained comfortably in camp, the weather was perfect, and nothing occurred to disturb the peace or enjoyment of the long voyage. Its only drawback lay in the monotony of water and forest, unrelieved by a sign of human presence, that constantly surrounded them.

As one of the last days of May drew toward its perfect close, two of the occupants of the leading boat reclined beneath a small awning and watched in silence the western splendor of the waning day,--that wonderful spectacle which is never twice the same and whose incomparable glories never grow stale by repetition. The elder of the two was Madam Rothsay, whose placid face indexed the kindly nature that could not refuse the pleadings of a loved one, even when they were for the undertaking of so wild an expedition as the present.

"Is it not exquisite, aunty?" finally exclaimed the younger of the two, a girl of eighteen, whose blue eyes and fair hair were strikingly contrasted with the warm tintings of a face on which sun and wind had plied their magic arts for many days.

"Yes, dear, it is indeed exquisite, and so wonderfully peaceful," replied Madam Rothsay.

"That is the one thing I object to," laughed the girl. "It is all so stupidly peaceful that I am getting tired of it, and long for a bit of excitement."

"But my dear Edith, if Sir Jeffry had not assured me that every portion of this journey might be made through a country that was perfectly peaceful, I should have never consented to undertake it. Besides, I thought you were quite tired of the excitements and gayety of New York. You certainly said so."

"Yes, so I was. That is, I was so tired of the stupid men one had so constantly to meet that I longed to get away to some place where they would not dare follow."

"I agree with you, my dear, that most of them were very stupid. There was Ensign Christie, for instance, who--"

"Now, aunty! you know I didn't mean him, or the men like him, who had done splendid things, and were just aching for a chance to do more. Besides, I am sure that if Mr. Christie had been possessed of the slightest desire to follow us, we could not have found any place in all the world where he would not dare venture. I meant such creatures as that absurd little paymaster, who talked about a stupid tub he had invented, until I couldn't help asking him why he didn't follow the example of the three wise men of Gotham and sail away in it."

"What did he answer?"

"Said he believed his old tub was quite seaworthy, and that he should be perfectly willing to undertake a voyage in it, provided it would lead him to me. Oh, he was so silly, and so pompous, and so conceited, and so spick and span! He is the most immaculate creature you ever saw, and was great fun for a while. Then he got to be such a desperate bore that I simply couldn't endure him any longer; and so, here we are."

"But I thought your sole reason for wanting to come out here was to see your father and Donald, and give them a joyful surprise."

"Of course, you dear goosey, that was the most chiefest of my reasons, as Willy Shakespeare would say, and I do so long to see them that it seems as though I couldn't wait until to-morrow evening. You said we would be there by this time to-morrow, you remember, Mr. Cuyler, and a promise is a promise, you know."

"I did say so, Miss Edith, and I think I may safely repeat my promise, provided we make camp a little later than usual this evening, and get started again by daylight to-morrow morning," answered the middle-aged lieutenant, who sat just back of the ladies and steered the boat. "Yon far-reaching land," he continued, "is Point Pelee, and from there the fort is only about twenty-five miles away."

"Then to-night's camp is to be our last," reflected Edith, soberly. "Well, I must confess that for some reasons I am sorry. I have so enjoyed the glorious camp-fires, and the singing, and the stories, and the stars, and the ripple of the water on the beach, and the sweet-scented balsam beds, and everything; haven't you, aunty?"

"Yes, dear. I suppose I have," replied Madam Rothsay. "But I am not sure that I shall not enjoy quite as much a substantial roof over my head, sitting at a regularly appointed table, and sleeping between sheets once more; for I take it such things are to be had, even in Detroit, are they not, Mr. Cuyler?"

"Yes, indeed, madam," replied the lieutenant. "You will find there all the necessities, as well as many of the luxuries of civilization; for Detroit is quite a metropolis, I assure you."

"Just fancy!" exclaimed Edith, "a metropolis buried a month deep in the wilderness. And I suppose the officers get up dances and receptions and excursions and boating parties, or something of that kind, very often?"

"All the time; and if they are not enjoying some of those things at this very minute, it is only because they await your coming to crown their festivities with completeness."

"Nonsense! They don't know we are coming."

"I beg your pardon, but Major Gladwyn was notified some months ago that he might expect the arrival of this expedition some time about the first of June."

"The expedition, yes; but us, no. We are to appear as a delightful surprise, you know. Oh dear! what fun it will be! By the way, Mr. Cuyler, are there many pretty girls in this forest metropolis?"

"I believe some of the native young ladies, both French and Indian, are considered quite attractive," replied the lieutenant, evasively.

"Oh, squaws! But they don't count, you know. I mean English or American girls."

"Do you make a distinction between the two?"

"Certainly. Aunty, here, is English, and I am American. Don't you notice a difference between us?" answered Miss Audacity, saucily.

"I can only note that each is more charming in her own way than the other," replied the lieutenant, gallantly.

Conversation was interrupted at this moment by the appearance of a beach suitable for a landing, and the heading of the boat toward it. A minute later it was run ashore, and the ladies were helped carefully out, while the remaining bateaux were beached on either side in quick succession.

A scene of orderly confusion immediately followed, as camp equipage of every description was taken from the boats and carried to the place where axemen were already at work clearing away underbrush or cutting wood for the fires. Every one was in the highest of spirits, and the gloomy forest rang with shouts and laughter; for was not this the last camp? and would not the morrow witness the completion of their arduous journey?

While their own little tent was being erected, the ladies, according to their custom, sought relief from the cramped positions and long confinement of the boat in a brisk walk up the beach. The darkening shadows warned them not to go as far as usual, and at the end of a few hundred yards they turned to retrace their steps.

Suddenly, without the warning of a sound to indicate a human presence, they were surrounded by half a dozen dusky forms, that seemed to spring from the very earth, their half-uttered cries were smothered by rude hands clapped over their mouths, and before they realized what had happened they were being hurried at a breathless pace through the blackness of the forest.

They were not taken far, but on the edge of a small glade, or natural opening, were allowed to sink at the foot of two trees, standing a yard or so apart. To these they were securely bound, and then, as mysteriously as they had appeared, their captors left them. So far as the terrified women could judge from the evidence of their senses, the forest was unpeopled save by themselves, though from the lake shore they could still hear the cheerful shouts of those engaged in preparing Cuyler's camp.

"Oh, my dear child! my poor dear child!" moaned the elder woman; "what does it all mean? Oh, it is too terrible! Too awful!"

"Hush, aunty," answered the girl. "We are in the hands of the savages, and God alone knows what our fate is to be. At any rate, we must keep clear-headed, and not give way to our feelings. I am thinking of those poor, unsuspecting men. If we could only warn them, they might be able to defend themselves, and possibly help us afterwards. Don't you think if we should both scream together that they would hear us?"

"Edith, child! are you crazy? We should be instantly killed. Not a sound, as you value your life!"

"I must, aunty. I should be ashamed to live if I failed to do the one thing of which I am capable."

With this the brave girl lifted her voice in a shrill cry for help, that echoed far and wide through the dim aisles of the forest; but it was too late, for at the same moment there came a crashing volley, mingled with savage yells, that announced an attack on the devoted camp.

CHAPTER XVIII
SURPRISE AND DESTRUCTION
OF THE BOAT BRIGADE

For many days had the scouts of Pontiac watched from the shore the boat brigade as it made its slow way toward Detroit. Night after night had they hovered about its camps, peering with greedy eyes from darkest shadows at the coveted wealth which the redcoats, ignorant of the presence of danger, so carelessly guarded. It was well to let the white men have the toil of bringing it as near the Indian villages as possible, and so an attack was not ordered until the very last night. Then the two hundred Wyandot warriors, detailed for the purpose, watched the boats until a landing was effected, silently surrounded the camp while everything was in confusion, and at a signal poured in their deadly fire.

To Cuyler's men this volley was as a thunderbolt from a clear sky. Never was a surprise more complete; never was overwhelming disaster more sudden. They were paralyzed and unnerved. A score fell at the first fire, and though Cuyler succeeded in forming the rest in an irregular semicircle about the boats, their return shots were so wildly scattering and ineffective that the enemy were emboldened to abandon their usual tactics, break from cover in a body, and rush fiercely upon the wavering line of panic-stricken soldiers. Most of these now saw Indians for the first time. None waited for a second glance, but flinging away their muskets, all ran madly for the boats.

Of these they succeeded in launching five, which were instantly filled beyond their capacity. So ill-directed were their efforts to escape, that the Indians, by setting two more boats afloat and starting in pursuit, easily overtook three of the fugitive craft, which surrendered to them without resistance. The remaining two, by hoisting sail and taking advantage of an off-shore breeze, made good their escape and were headed in the direction of Sandusky on the opposite side of the lake. In one of these was the commander of the ill-fated expedition, who had been the last man to leave the beach.

Wild with joy over a victory so easily gained and so rich in results, the Indians, after securing their prisoners, lighted great fires, and, gathered about these, abandoned themselves to feasting and drinking. Among the captured supplies was a quantity of liquor, upon which they pounced with avidity. Heads of kegs were broken in, and the fiery stuff was recklessly quaffed from cups, vessels of birch bark, or anything that would hold it; some even scooping it up in their hands, until all became filled with the madness of demons. They danced, yelled, waved aloft their bloody scalps, and fought like wild beasts, while the trembling captives, crouching in scattered groups, seemed to hear their own death knell in every whoop.

One such scene of hideous revelry was enacted in the little glade beside which Madam Rothsay and Edith Hester had been left helplessly bound by their captors. From the moment of the girl's brave effort to warn the camp, these two had listened with straining ears to the babel of sounds by which the whole course of the tragedy was made plain to them. They shuddered at the volleys, at the screams of the wounded, and at the triumphant yells of the victors. They almost forgot their own wretched position in their horror at the fate of their recent companions. But when all was over, and the hideous revelry of the savages was begun within their sight, a realization of their own misery returned with overwhelming force, and they again trembled at the possibilities of their fate. A number of squaws had accompanied this war party, and they could see these busily engaged securing and concealing what weapons they could find at the very beginning of the debauch.

"Even those creatures realize the dreadful things that are likely to happen, and are taking what precautions they may to guard against them," moaned Madam Rothsay.

"Yes," replied Edith, "and now, if ever, is our time to escape. Oh, if we were not so helplessly bound and could slip away into the woods! I would rather die in an effort to escape than suffer the agony of this suspense. Can't you loosen your arms one little bit, aunty?"

As the girl spoke she strained at her own bonds until they sunk deep into her tender flesh, but without loosening them in the slightest.

The elder woman also struggled for a moment with all her strength, and then sank back with a groan.

"I can't, Edith! It's no use, and only hurts. No, we can do nothing save commend ourselves to God and trust to his mercy. Oh, my poor child! My poor dear child!"

The fires blazed higher, the maddening liquor flowed like water, the yells grew fiercer, and the dancing more furious. The lurid scene became a very pandemonium, and the leaping forms of the savages seemed those of so many devils. The captive women closed their eyes to shut out the horrid picture.

Suddenly Edith uttered a stifled scream--a warm breath was on her neck, and a soft voice was whispering words of comfort in her ear:--

"Hush! Do not scream. Do not fear. You shall be saved. I am Ah-mo, daughter of Pontiac, the great chief, sent by my father to see that you are not harmed. Now I will take you away. It is not safe for you longer to remain in this place. There. Do not rise. You would be seen. Move yourself carefully into the shadow behind the tree."

As these words were uttered, Edith's bonds were severed; she felt that she was again free, and, filled with courage born of a new hope, she obeyed implicitly the directions of her unseen friend. As she gained the shadow she found herself beside a girlish figure, who placed a finger on her lips, and then in a whisper bade her speak to Madam Rothsay, that she might not be frightened into an outcry. This Edith did, the elder woman was released as she had been, and in another minute the freed captives, trembling with excitement and nearly suffocated by the intensity of their emotions, were following, hand in hand, their silently flitting guide in the direction of the lake shore.

Their escape was effected none too soon, for they were not gone a hundred yards when it occurred to one of the Indians who had captured them to take a look at his prizes. His listless saunter toward where he had left them was changed to movements of bewildered activity, as in place of the cowering captives, he found only severed thongs, and realized that in some mysterious manner a release had been effected. He uttered a yell that brought a number of his companions to the spot, and in another minute a score or so of half-sobered savages were ranging the forest in every direction like sleuth-hounds.

"We must run!" exclaimed the Indian girl, as her quick ear caught the significant cries announcing the discovery of the escape.

Now the flight became a panting scramble over logs and through bushes. Fortunately the shore was near at hand, for Madam Rothsay was ready to sink from exhaustion as they reached it.

A low, bird-like call from Ah-mo brought to the beach a canoe that had rested motionless a few rods from shore. It held but a single occupant, and as it lightly touched the beach the Indian girl hurriedly assisted her breathless companions to enter, gave it a vigorous shove, took her own place in the stern, and seizing a paddle aided in its rapid but noiseless flight over the dark waters. The moon had not yet risen; and so, favored by darkness, a few vigorous strokes served to place the light craft beyond eyesight of those on shore. It seemed, though, as if the savages whose angry voices they could hear from the very spot of beach they had just left must see it, and the escaped captives hardly breathed as they reflected upon the narrow margin of safety by which they were separated from their fierce pursuers. All at once there came from these a yell of triumph instantly succeeded by the sounds of a struggle and followed a minute later by cries of rejoicing.

As these sounds receded from the shore, and the canoe began once more to move forward under the impetus of its noiseless paddles, Ah-mo leaned forward and whispered to Edith, who sat nearest her: "They have taken some new captive. Perhaps it is the commander."

"Oh, I hope not!" murmured the girl. "I hope it is not poor Mr. Cuyler." At the thought a great wave of pity welled up in her heart. She knew the terrible hopelessness of a captivity in those hands; and though she could not yet determine whether she were still a prisoner or not, her present position was blissful compared with what it had been a few minutes before.

If she had known the cause of those wild shouts of rejoicing, and who it was that had been made captive in her place, her heart would indeed have been heavy, but mercifully the knowledge was spared to her.

In the canoe the ladies found several of their own wraps and cushions that Ah-mo had been thoughtful enough to secure. In these they nestled together for warmth and comfort, and talking in low tones discussed their situation during the hours that the canoe sped steadily onward.

At length the moon rose, and turning her head, Edith gazed curiously at the girl behind her. She could see that she was slender and very graceful, and she imagined her to be beautiful.

"How did your father know of our coming, and why did he send you to care for us?" she asked at length.

"My father is a great chief, and his eyes are everywhere," answered Ah-mo, proudly. "He sent me and Atoka, my brother, because he feared you might come to harm at the hands of the Wyandots."

"But why should he be particularly interested in our welfare, more than in that of others?"

"Are you not the daughter of Two Trees, the white-haired major, and is he not the friend of Pontiac? Even now he dwells in the camp of my father."

"Do you mean my father, Major Hester?" cried the bewildered girl.

"Yes."

"But he can't be dwelling among the enemies of the English. You must be mistaken, Ah-mo."

"It is as I have said," replied the girl.

"Are you then taking us to him now?"

"No. It would not be safe. There are too many bad men even in the camps of the Ottawas, and my father would have the daughter of his friend removed from all harm."

"Where, then, are you going?"

"You soon will see."

And with this the white girl was forced to be content.

The night was nearly spent when the canoe approached a small island in the middle of Lake Erie, but commanding the mouth of the Detroit river. Here it was run into a cove, and beached beside several other similar craft. Atoka, the young Indian, who had spoken no word during all this time, uttered a peculiar cry as he sprang ashore, and directly several dark forms appeared from a thicket that bordered the beach.

Ah-mo assured Edith that from these men she had nothing to fear, as they were picked Ottawa warriors devoted to her father's interests, and stationed them as outlooks to report the movements of any vessels on the lake.

After a few minutes of lively conversation between them and Atoka, the whole party entered the thicket, where, snugly hidden, stood several Indian lodges. One of these was quickly made ready for the women, and here, in spite of the uncertainties of their situation, Madam Rothsay and Edith Hester, wrapped in their own shawls, soon fell into the slumber of utter exhaustion.

CHAPTER XIX
THE TOTEM SAVES DONALD'S LIFE

Exhausted as she was, Edith Hester would hardly have slept that night had she known that he whose capture was the direct result of her flight was her own dearly loved brother Donald; but so it was. By strenuous exertions, he had so expedited the movements of his own party that they had passed two, and sometimes three, of Cuyler's camping-places in a day. They always examined these for information concerning those whom they were so anxious to overtake, and after a while their anxiety was increased by the finding of traces of Indian scouts in and about every camping-place. At length the camp sites gave proof of having been so recently occupied, that it seemed as though they might sight Cuyler's boats at any time, and Paymaster Bullen, in anticipation of a speedy meeting with the ladies, devoted so much attention to his personal appearance that never had such a dandy as he been seen in the wilderness.

As the paymaster's efforts to enhance his personal attractions increased, Donald's ever-growing anxiety led him to become more than ever impatient of such things and eager to hasten forward. He became provoked at his companion's frivolity, and regretted ever having consented to travel with him. When he finally discovered the prints of Indian moccasins about one of Cuyler's fires, the ashes of which were still hot, he grew so apprehensive of evil, and so impatient to get on, that he refused to allow his crew even the scanty half-hour of rest at noon to which they were accustomed. He so urged their labors of this day, by alternate threats and promises, that the canoe reached the eastern side of Point au Pelee at the very time of Cuyler's landing on its western shore. Here Donald informed his men that they might cook their evening meal, and rest for two hours, at the end of which time they must be prepared to push on, as he was determined to overtake the other party before they broke camp on the morrow.

During the preparation of supper, the young man paced restlessly up and down the beach, casting occasional scornful glances at the dapper little paymaster, who, with the assistance of the faithful "Tummas," was taking his regular evening bath, in his beloved tub.

While matters stood thus, there came a sound so startling and of such vital import that all paused in their employment and held their breath to listen. It was the cry of a woman in distress, faint and distant, but unmistakable. Half uttered, it was cut short by a crash of guns, mingled with savage war-whoops, that proclaimed as clearly as words the state of affairs on the opposite side of that narrow neck of land.

In an instant, Donald Hester, so frenzied by his sister's appeal for aid as to be well-nigh unconscious of his own movements, seized his rifle, plunged into the forest, and was dashing recklessly in the direction of the ominous sounds.

The Senecas, whom he thus left to their own devices, and who had long been expecting some such moment, acted with almost equal promptness in making prisoners of the two remaining white men. A few minutes of animated discussion as to what should be done with them ensued. All were impatient to join their fellow savages, and share in the spoils of their certain victory, to which they also wished to add their own trophies. But what should be done with the white medicine man? He was too fat to be urged at speed through the forest. They feared to kill him, for they believed him to be of a weak mind, and therefore under the direct protection of the Great Spirit. Besides, being bald-headed, he could furnish no scalp, and was therefore not worth killing.

In this dilemma, the Zebra conceived an idea which his companions greeted with grunts of approval, and immediately proceeded to carry out. A few minutes later the horrified paymaster, as naked as when he was born, was seated in his own bathtub, precariously maintaining his balance, and floating away before a gentle off-shore breeze, over the vast watery solitude of Lake Erie.

As the Indians watched him, until he was but a white speck in the gathering gloom, they reasoned that if he were indeed a medicine man he could take care of himself; if he were crazy, the Great Spirit would protect him. And if he were merely an ordinary mortal he would surely be drowned; while, in no case, would blame be attached to them.

Then they gathered up his half-dozen precious wigs, all of which had been laid

At War with Pontiac

out for inspection, that their owner might decide in which one he should appear before the ladies, but which the Indians only regarded as so many scalps; concealed the canoe, together with much of their newly acquired property, and started toward the scene of battle. Two stalwart warriors, seizing the unfortunate and bewildered "Tummas" by the shoulders, rushed him along at breathless speed, occasionally urging him to greater exertions by suggestive pricks from the sharp points of their knives.

Although Donald had started to the assistance of his imperilled sister with a recklessness that disregarded all the traditions of woodcraft, he came to his senses as he drew near the scene of recent conflict, and thereafter no forest warrior could have proceeded with greater stealth than he.

The short fight was over, the prisoners were secured, many fires had been lighted, and the deadly work of the fire-water was already begun. With a heavy heart and a sickening dread, the young soldier crept noiselessly from one lighted circle to another, narrowly escaping discovery a dozen times, and scanning anxiously each dejected group of captives. All were men, nor could he anywhere catch a glimpse of feminine draperies. At one place he saw a confused group, of what he fancied might be captives, on the opposite side of a fire-lighted opening, and made a great circuit through the woods in order to approach it more closely.

Suddenly there arose a clamor of voices, and, as though aware of his presence, a score of savages, some of them holding aloft blazing firebrands, came running through the forest directly toward him. There was no time for flight, and he could only fling himself flat beside the trunk of a prostrate tree, up to which he had just crawled, ere they were upon him. A dozen warriors passed him, leaping over both the log and the crouching figure behind it. He was beginning to cherish a hope that all might do so; but such good fortune was not to be his. Another, who bore a flaming brand, slipped as he bounded over the obstruction. A shower of blazing embers fell on Donald's head and bare neck. Maddened by pain, he sprang to his feet, dealt the stumbling savage a blow that knocked him flat, and turned to fly for his life. As he did so, he was grappled by two others, and though he struggled so furiously that he managed to fling them both from him, the delay was fatal. A moment later he was borne to the earth by overwhelming numbers.

When again allowed to rise it was as a pinioned prisoner, bruised and breathless. With exulting shouts, his captors dragged him into the circle of firelight, and when they saw that he was not one of Cuyler's men, but a newcomer, they were extravagant in their joy. They were also furious against him on account of the escape of the women captives, in which it was supposed he had been instrumental. Half-crazed with drink as they were, they determined that he should pay the penalty for this offence then and there.

"Let the palefaced dog roast in the flames!"

"Burn him!"

"Fling him into the fire!"

"He has sought our company; let us give him a warm welcome!"

"It will be a lesson to others of his kind not to meddle with our prisoners!"

"Let him feel that the vengeance of the Wyandots is sudden and awful!"

These, with many similar cries, rent the night air, and though Donald understood no word of what was said, he knew from the savage expression of the faces crowding about him that he was to suffer some dreadful fate, and nerved himself to bear it.

If he must die, it should be as became one of his race and training. But, oh! it was hard! He was so young, so full of life and hope. Could he hold out to the bitter end? Yes, he must. He had chosen to be a soldier. He was a soldier. Other soldiers had met their death by savage torture and faced it bravely. What they had done, he must do. But was there no help for him, none at all? As he searched the scowling faces of those who thronged about him, reviling, taunting, and revelling in his despair, he saw no trace of mercy, no pity, no gleam of hope. He knew that there was no help.

With it all, there was one consolation. He could discover no sign of his beloved sister. She, at least, would be spared the sight of his torments. She might even by some miracle have escaped.

They dragged him roughly, and with maudlin shoutings, to a small tree that stood by itself, and bound him to it with so many lashings that only his head was free to move. Then they heaped dry wood about him, piling it up until it was above his waist.

He knew now what he was to be called upon to endure. No words were needed to tell him that he was to be burned alive, and he prayed that they would pile the wood higher, that death might come the more quickly. But some among his tormentors thought it was already too high, and in their desire to prolong his sufferings they tore away a portion of the pile. Others insisted that it was not enough, and attempted to build it higher; and so they wrangled among themselves, until one, to settle the dispute, ran for a blazing brand and thrust it among the faggots that still remained.

By this time, news of what was taking place had spread abroad, and many from other scenes of revelry came running to participate in this new diversion. As a bright blaze leaped through the crackling wood and revealed distinctly the pallid face of the victim, there was first a yell of delight and then a great hush of expectancy, while all watched eagerly to see how he would bear the first touch of flame.

At this moment, there came a commotion in the crowd. A single figure, with face hideously painted in narrow stripes, broke from it, sprang forward, and dashing aside the blazing wood, shouted a few words in a tongue that was strange to most of them, though some understood. These translated what was said to the others, and in a few seconds every warrior was repeating in awed tones to his neighbor:--

"He is of the Metai! He is of the Totem of the Bear! The mark is on his arm! If he dies at our hands, then shall we feel the wrath of the magic circle!"

In a moment Donald's hunting-shirt was stripped from him, his left arm was bared, and at sight of the indelible signet thus exposed a great fear fell upon the savages. At once those who had been most eager for the death of the prisoner, became foremost in friendly offices that they hoped might banish their offence from his mind, and Donald breathed a prayer of thankfulness for his wonderful deliverance.

CHAPTER XX
BITTER DISAPPOINTMENT AT FORT DETROIT

The month elapsed since Donald left Detroit had been to the imprisoned garrison of that important post a period of gloom and incessant anxiety. Although, after the first outbreak, no general attack had been made on the place, the rigor of its siege had not for a moment been relaxed. It was seldom that an Indian was to be seen; but if a soldier exposed himself above the walls or at a loop-hole, the venomous hiss of a bullet instantly warned him of his peril, and of the tireless vigilance of the unseen foe. Provisions became so scarce that every ounce of food was carefully collected in one place, kept under guard, and sparingly doled out each morning. The faces of men and women grew wan and pinched with hunger, while the children clamored incessantly for food. If it had not been for the brave aid of a French farmer, dwelling across the river, who occasionally, on dark nights, smuggled scanty supplies to the beleaguered garrison, they would have been forced by starvation to a surrender.

In all this time no man slept, save in his clothes, and with a gun by his side. Night alarms were frequent, and only incessant watchfulness averted the destruction of the place by fire, from arrows tipped with blazing tow, that fell at all hours, with greater or less frequency, on the thatched roofs within the palisades.

With all this, there was no thought of yielding in the minds of Gladwyn or his men. The red cross of St. George still floated proudly above them, and each evening the sullen boom of the sunset gun echoed defiantly across the waters of the broad river.

While the Indians could not be induced to attempt a general assault upon the slight defences, in spite of its prospects of almost certain success, Pontiac so skilfully disposed his forces that not only was the fort under constant watch, but no one could approach it in any direction without discovery. They, too, collected all the provisions within their reach, purchasing quantities from the Canadians, and gathering them in the commodious house that still held Major Hester a prisoner-guest. Eagerly as the besieged watched for reinforcements and supplies, the Indians were no less keenly on the lookout for the same things.

Knowing that Cuyler's expedition must have started from Fort Niagara, Major Gladwyn despatched the schooner that bore his name down the lake, to intercept, warn, and hasten it. The narrowly escaped capture by a great fleet of canoes, as she lay becalmed at the mouth of the river, and was only saved by the springing up of a timely breeze. She failed to discover the object of her search, and finally reached the Niagara without having delivered her warning.

It was now time for her return, while Cuyler should have arrived long since; and day after day were the eyes of the weary garrison directed down the shining river, in efforts to detect the first glint of sails or flash of oars.

While matters stood thus, there came, late one afternoon, a loud cry, announcing joyful tidings, from the sentinel on one of the river bastions. His shout was taken up and repeated by all who happened to be on the water front, and in a minute the whole place was astir. The inhabitants poured into the narrow streets and hastened to the river's edge, their haggard faces lighted with a new hope and their eager voices exchanging the welcome news. The long-expected reinforcements had come at last. The boats were in sight. They had escaped the perils of their journey and were safely arrived. Now the danger was over, and all would again be well with Detroit.

As the motley throng of soldiers, in soiled uniforms, traders, voyageurs, pale-faced women, and wondering children, streamed to the narrow beach beyond the water gate, all could see the approaching boats as, in long-extended line and with flashing oars, one after another rounded the last wooded point and advanced slowly up the river.

From the stern of the foremost boat flew the red flag of England. As it drew near, cheer after cheer broke from the excited garrison, while from the rampart above them a loud-voiced cannon boomed forth it assurance that the fort still held out.

Alas, for the high hopes of the stout defenders! Their joy was quickly quenched; for when the long column of eighteen boats was in full view, and the rejoicing was at its height, dark, naked figures suddenly leaped up, with brandished weapons and exulting yells, in every boat. The fierce war-whoop came quavering over the water, and in a moment the dreadful truth was known. The entire convoy had been captured, and was in the enemy's hands.

As the mournful procession of boats moved past, though well over toward the opposite bank of the river, the disheartened garrison saw that each was rowed by two or more white captives, who were guarded and forced to their labor by armed savages. As the heavy-hearted spectators were about to turn away from this distressing sight, a thrilling incident absorbed their attention, and held them spellbound.

The last boat contained four white men and but three Indians. One of the former was Donald Hester, and he it was who steered. Although he had been well treated by his captors, after the mystic marking on his arm to which the Zebra attracted their attention had saved him from an awful death, he was still held a close prisoner, and was still uncertain as to the fate reserved for him. This, however, concerned him little. Nothing could be worse than the mental suffering he had already undergone, and his present anxiety was only for his sister Edith. What had become of her? Where was she, and by what perils was she surrounded? He became frantic as he reflected upon her helplessness and the restraints that prevented him from flying to her assistance. He had learned from his fellow-captives that nothing had been seen of her nor of her companion after the attack on Cuyler's camp, and also that two boats, containing many fugitives, had effected an escape. She must then be in one of those, and if she were, what might she not be suffering, without food or shelter, and liable at any moment to fall into the hands of some roving band of savages? For her sake, he must regain his freedom. Yes, he must, and he would. Why not strike for it at that very moment? Would he ever have a better chance?

As the last boat came abreast of the schooner, surging at her cables not more than a quarter of a mile away, Donald called out in English to the rowers in his boat that each should seize one of the Indian guards and throw him overboard, while he would stand ready to aid any one, or all of them, in the undertaking.

The soldier nearest him replied that he feared he had not the requisite strength.

"Very well," said Donald; "pretend exhaustion and change places with me."

As this order was obeyed and the young ensign stepped forward, as though to take his comrade's place, he suddenly seized hold of an unsuspecting Indian, lifted him bodily, and flung him into the river. At the same moment the savage clutched his assailant's clothing, and as he cleared the boat dragged Donald after him over its side. The two remaining Indians, seized with a panic, leaped overboard and struck out for shore, while the three soldiers, bending to their oars, directed their craft with desperate energy toward the schooner, followed by a storm of bullets and a dozen canoes.

In the meantime, Donald and his antagonist, swept away by the current, were engaged in a frightful struggle for life and death, now rising gasping to the surface, then sinking to unknown depths, but always grappling, and clutching at each other's throat.

At length, when it seemed to the white lad that he had spent an eternity in the cruel green depths, when his ears were bursting and his eyes starting from their sockets, he found himself once more at the surface, breathing in great gulps of the blessed air, and alone. For a moment he could not believe it, but gazed wildly about him, expecting each instant to feel the awful clutch that should again drag him under. He was nearly exhausted, and so weak that had not a floating oar come within his reach he must quickly have sunk, to rise no more.

Clinging feebly to that Heaven-sent bit of wood, he kept his face above the water while his spent strength was gradually restored.

At the boom of a cannon, he lifted his head a little higher, and looked back. A cloud of blue smoke was drifting away from the now distant schooner, a boat was alongside, and a fleet of canoes was scurrying out of range. His recent companions had then escaped, and pursuit of them had so attracted the attention of the Indians that none had given him a thought. They doubtless never questioned but what that death grapple in the water had resulted fatally to both contestants. So much the better for him. No search would be made, and he might escape, after all. And dear Edith! At length he was free to go in search of her. With this thought the lad took a new hold on life, grasped his friendly oar more firmly, and tried to plan some course of action.

Making no motion that might attract hostile attention, he drifted passively, until the sun had set in a flood of glory, and the stars peeped timidly down at him from their limitless heights. By this time he was some miles below the fort, and near the eastern bank of the river. Though he had seen many canoes pass up stream, at a distance so great that he was not noticed, there was now neither sign nor sound of human presence, and very gently the young soldier began to swim toward land. How blessed it was to touch bottom again, then to drag himself cautiously and wearily into a clump of tall sedges, and lie once more on the substantial bosom of mother earth. For an hour or more he slept, and then, greatly refreshed, he awoke to renewed activity.

CHAPTER XXI
IN SEARCH OF A LOST SISTER

Donald had no difficulty in finding the broad trail that connected all the widely scattered Indian villages on the east bank of the river, and when he reached it he instinctively turned to the south. The main body of the enemy lay to the northward, and to proceed in that direction would be the height of folly. There was still one small camp below him, as Donald knew from having seen it that morning when on his way up the river, and to this he determined to go. He needed food, clothing, arms, and a canoe. All of these might be obtained in an Indian camp, as well as elsewhere, if only one dared go in search of them and possessed the skill necessary to secure them. Much also would depend on chance; but, after his recent experiences, the young soldier felt assured that he had been born under a propitious star. At any rate, he was ready to do and dare anything in furtherance of his present plan, and so he set forth at a brisk pace in search of some source of supplies.

He had covered several miles with every sense keenly alert, but without detecting an indication of human presence, when he suddenly smelled an Indian encampment. He could neither see nor hear anything of it, but no one having once recognized the pungent odor, combined of smoke, skins, furs, freshly peeled bark, dried grasses, and decayed animal matter, that lingers about the rude dwellings of all savage races, could ever mistake it for anything else. A single faint whiff of this, borne to Donald, on a puff of the night wind, gave him the very knowledge he wanted, and he at once began to move with the same caution that he had observed on the previous evening while creeping up to the fire-lighted circles of the victorious Wyandots.

It was perilous business, this venturing into a camp of hostile Indians through the darkness, but Donald reflected that it would be even worse by daylight. He also argued, that while success in his proposed thieving would mean everything to him, he could not be worse off than he was a few hours since, even if he failed and was captured. So he crept forward with the noiseless motions of a serpent, until the conical lodges were plainly in view by the dim light of smoldering camp-fires.

At War with Pontiac

There was one feature of this camp that greatly puzzled our young woodsman, and that was its silence. Surely the night was too young for all the inmates of those lodges to have retired, and yet there was no sound of voices. Not even the wail of a child was to be heard nor the barking of a dog. It was unaccountable, and gave Donald a creepy feeling that he tried in vain to shake off. He moved with an even greater caution than if he had been guided by the usual sounds of such a place and spent a full hour in examining the camp from all points before daring to enter it.

At length he detected a faint muttering in one of the lodges and a reply to it; but both voices were those of querulous age. A moment later the tottering figure of an old man emerged from the lodge, and crouching beside a dying fire threw on a few sticks with shaking hands and drew his blanket more closely about his shrunken form.

In an instant a full meaning of the situation flashed into Donald's mind. The camp was deserted of all except the infirm and very aged. All the others--men, women, children, and even the very dogs--had gone to participate in the festivities of the up-river camps to which so many white prisoners had that day been taken. He shuddered to contemplate the nature of these festivities,--the tortures, the anguish, and the fearful tragedies that would furnish their entertainment; but he no longer hesitated to enter this deserted camp and appropriate such of its properties as suited his fancy.

From the very fire beside which the old man crouched and shivered, he took a blazing brand and using it to light his way entered the lodge from which the former had emerged. It seemed empty of everything save that in one corner, on a heap of dried grasses, there lay an old wrinkled hag, who stared at him with keen beady eyes, and then set up a shrill screaming that caused him to beat a hasty retreat.

He fared better in other lodges, some of which were empty of inmates, and some occupied by persons too aged or ill to harm him. These either cowered trembling before him, or spit at and reviled him with distorted features and gestures of impotent rage. It was an unpleasant task, this taking advantage of helplessness to walk off with other people's property; but under the circumstances it seemed to Donald right, and he was soon clad in the complete buckskin costume of a warrior, besides having accumulated a comfortable store of provisions. He was grievously disappointed at not discovering a rifle, nor indeed a firearm of any kind, and being obliged to put up with a hunting-knife as his sole weapon. Still, on the whole, he had so little cause for complaint that as he left the camp and made his way to the landing where he hoped to find a canoe he congratulated himself upon his good fortune.

It seemed to fail him, however, at the river-bank; for, search as he might, he could not find a canoe nor a craft of any kind. Now, he was indeed in a quandary. It would be worse than useless to return to the Indian camp, that might at any moment be repeopled. He dared not go up the river, for that way lay the hosts of Pontiac; nor could he cross it and make his way to the fort. There was obviously but one course to pursue, which was to keep on down stream until he had put a safe distance between himself and the Indian camp, and then to wait for daylight by which to resume his search for a canoe.

This he did, first wading for a long distance in the shallow water close to shore to conceal his trail, and then plodding sturdily ahead through the bewildering darkness of the forest for hours, until finally, overcome by exhaustion, he sank down at the foot of a great tree and almost instantly fell asleep.

When Donald next awoke, stiff and aching in every joint, the rising sun warned him that he must lose no time in placing a greater distance between himself and those who would soon be on his trail, if, indeed, the pursuit were not already begun. So he set off at a brisk pace, still keeping the general southerly direction on which he had determined until he should reach the lake. He had not walked more than two hours, and was staying his stomach with a handful of parched corn brought from the Indian camp, when, all at once, he found himself amid the remains of recent camp-fires on ground that was much trampled. It was the very scene of his capture by the Wyandots and of his narrow escape from death. Yes, there was the identical tree to which he had been bound. Turning, with a shudder, he hastened from the place of such horrid memories, and instinctively retraced his course of two nights before across the narrow neck of land that had proved fatal to so many of his countrymen, and on which the dear sister whom he now sought had last been seen.

Reaching the eastern side of the point, and skirting the shore for a short distance, he came upon another place of camping, which he instantly recognized as the spot where he had left Paymaster Bullen.

"Poor old Bullen!" he reflected half aloud. "I wonder what he thought of my deserting him the way I did; and I also wonder what became of him. I suppose he must be dead long before this, and 'Tummas,' too, poor fellow; for I didn't see anything of them among the prisoners yesterday. I never trusted those Senecas; but Wilkins was so cocksure of them that he wouldn't listen to a word against them. Wonder what he'll say now. I wouldn't be here at this moment, though, if it hadn't been for that fellow, 'Zebra,' as Bullen called him. Queer how things turn out in this funny old world! I only wish I knew just what that tattooing on my arm means, and what the Metai is, anyway. If I did, I might turn the knowledge to advantage. Hello! Something has been carried into those bushes,--the paymaster's tub for a guinea."

During his soliloquy the young woodsman's trained eye rested on a broken twig and a bit of bruised bark at the edge of a near-by thicket. Stepping to the place and parting the bushes, he uttered a cry of joy. There, bottom-side up, and imperfectly concealed, as though in great haste, lay the canoe in which he had so recently journeyed. Beneath it he found a rifle that had belonged to the paymaster, as well as most of his luggage, which included a good supply of ammunition, provisions, and cooking-utensils. In fact, nearly everything that the canoe had contained was there excepting its passengers and the redoubtable tub.

"The disappearance of that tub is the strangest thing of all," muttered Donald, as, exulting in this sudden wealth, he hastened to build a fire and make the cup of coffee for which he was longing. "What reason could the beggars have had for lugging it off? and why didn't I see something of it in the boats yesterday? Too bad about Bullen, though, for he was a good fellow in spite of his crotchets."

The daring plan that forced itself in Donald's mind the minute he saw that canoe was to cross Lake Erie in it to Sandusky. There he would certainly learn what had become of Cuyler and those who escaped with him. Perhaps he would even find Edith there.

He was off the moment he had finished the hearty breakfast that restored his strength, his confidence in himself and his belief that everything was about to turn out for the best, after all. Nor did his good fortune desert him, for the broad surface of the great lake was as peaceful as a mill-pond all that day; the light breeze that ruffled it was so directly in his favor that he was enabled to aid his paddle with a sail, and at sunset he was nearing the southern coast. Camping where he landed, he cooked, ate, and slept, starting again at break of day for Sandusky, full of hope and anticipations of a warm welcome in that stout little post.

The sun was barely an hour high when he reached his destination, only to find a mass of charred and desolate ruins, that told with a mute eloquence of the fate that had overtaken Sandusky.

CHAPTER XXII
AMID THE RUINS OF FORT SANDUSKY

To discover only ruin, desolation, and death, instead of the cheery greetings of friends and the longed-for intelligence of Edith's safety that he had so confidently expected to gain at Sandusky, was so bitter a disappointment as to be bewildering, and it was some time ere Donald could do aught save wander like one who is dazed, among the melancholy ruins. He recalled his pleasant reception by Ensign Paully, the commanding officer, only a month before, when he had stopped there on his way down the lake, the cheerful evening he had spent in the mess-room, and the hopeful conversation concerning the settlement soon to be made near the sturdy little post. Now all that remained were great heaps of ashes and half-burned logs, gaunt chimneys, and a score of bodies, stripped, mutilated, and decomposed beyond recognition. The presence of these, and the fact that all of them were scalped, showed the destruction of the post to be the work of savages and not the voluntary act of its garrison; otherwise Donald might have hoped that the place had been abandoned and a retreat made to some stronger position.

Not only was the story of the tragedy plainly to be read in the mute evidences abounding on all sides, but the young woodsman was able to determine from the drift of ashes, the indentations of raindrops, and other distinct signs, just how many days had elapsed since the king's flag last waved above Sandusky. He found traces showing that Cuyler with his fugitives had been there since the destruction of the place, and from his own feelings he could readily imagine what theirs must have been.

These things he learned as easily as from a printed page; but with all his art he could gain no inkling of the information he most desired. Were his sister and Madam Rothsay among those who had escaped with Cuyler? In vain did he scan the prints of moccasined and booted feet, that abounded among the ruins. None was dainty enough to be that of a lady.

While Donald was bending over some footprints beside a small field-piece that, dismounted and rusted, lay half buried in ashes, a sudden whir-r-r caused him to spring back as though he had received an electric shock. Only his quickness saved him from the living death held in the fangs of a rattlesnake that had evidently just crawled from the black muzzle of the gun. The snake instantly re-coiled to repeat its venomous stroke, and though Donald could easily have killed it as he had scores of its kind, the presence of this hideous and sole representative of life in that place of the dead so filled him with horror that he turned and fled to his canoe. Nor did he pause in his flight until he had covered many miles of water, and was compelled to do so by the faintness of hunger.

He had instinctively shaped his course to the eastward, and now reason decided him to continue it in that direction. It was the only one that Cuyler could have taken, and in searching for his sister the young ensign had no other clue to follow save that afforded by the fugitives.

Coasting the shore until he discovered the mouth of a small stream, Donald forced his canoe up this until it was effectually concealed from the lake. Then he made a fire of dry wood that would give forth little smoke, and cooked the noontide meal, that was for that day his breakfast as well. Before it was finished he had decided to remain in his present place of concealment until nightfall, in order to have the aid of darkness in avoiding such Indians as might be travelling up or down the coast. Having satisfied his hunger, and extinguished his modest fire, he stationed himself at the foot of a great oak on the shore, where he commanded a good view of the lake and was at the same time well hidden from it. Here he reflected upon all that had happened, wondered if Cuyler had reached Presque Isle, if so, whether Edith and Christie had met, and tried to imagine the meeting, until at length he fell asleep and dreamed that Presque Isle was destroyed and that he was searching for traces of Edith in its ashes.

When he awoke, the sound of voices was in his ears, and for a moment it seemed as though his waking was but a continuation of his dream. Within a stone's-throw of where he lay barely hidden by a slight screen of leaves, a fleet of canoes was moving to the eastward, the very direction he must take if he adhered to his original plan. He counted ten, twenty, thirty, and believed that some had already passed when he awoke. They were filled with warriors, all armed and decked with war-paint of vermilion and black. There were a few squaws; but no children, no dogs, and but slight camp equipage. It was evidently a war-party, and a strong one.

Donald lay motionless, hardly daring to breathe, and watched them out of sight. Were they in pursuit of Cuyler and his handful of fugitives? were they on their way to attack Christie in his little fort? or were they in search of him to avenge his looting of the Wyandot lodges? This last thought was dismissed as quickly as formed; for, of course, no party of that size would be in pursuit of an individual, no matter how important he was or what he had done. No; they must be bound for Presque Isle, with the hope of picking up Cuyler on the way.

As the youth was in the very act of rising to go to the beach for a parting glimpse of the fleet, a movement on the water warned him to sink back just in time to escape the keen glances of the occupants of a single canoe, that seemed to have been left behind and to be in haste to overtake the main body. Besides the four Indians who paddled it, this canoe held a fifth, seated luxuriously in an object so unusual and startling that Donald almost uttered an exclamation at sight of it. "It could not be!" Donald rubbed his eyes and looked again. Yes, it was. There was no mistaking its shape or color.

"Bullen's tub, as I'm a sinner!" muttered the young man, under his breath. "If that doesn't beat everything! Where did they get it? What are they going to do with it? and what has become of its owner? Poor old chap! He can't possibly be alive, for he would have died rather than be parted from it. Now, though, I had better keep quiet for awhile and see what is coming next."

Although it lacked two hours of sunset, and Donald maintained his lonely watch until then, nothing more came in sight. He prepared another meal to strengthen him for a night of toil, and as soon as darkness had set in, made a start. Keeping so far out on the lake that the shore was but a dim line, he urged the canoe forward with his utmost strength through the solemn stillness of the long hours. He did not venture near shore until the eastern sky was paling with approaching dawn. Then, though he sought anxiously for some friendly stream in which to conceal his canoe, he failed to find one before the growing light warned him that it was no longer safe to remain on the water. He was thus forced to land on the open beach, and with great labor drag his craft up a steep bank to a hiding-place in the forest beyond. After that, with infinite pain, and moving backward as his work progressed, he carefully obliterated all traces of his landing by sweeping them with a bunch of twigs.

While certain that he must have passed the Indian fleet during the night, and that it would in turn pass him before the day was ended, he was compelled by utter weariness to sleep, which he did in a dense thicket at some distance from where he had hidden the canoe. When he awoke, it was so late in the day that he feared the savages had gone by, but after a while he again heard their voices, and peering from his covert again saw the entire fleet sweep past. This time he counted its occupants as well as he could, and discovered that the war-party numbered something over two hundred members. On this occasion the canoe containing the paymaster's tub was in the foremost rank, and there were no stragglers.

It was a great relief to the anxious watcher to catch this glimpse of the enemy and thus gain an approximate knowledge of their whereabouts, and after they had disappeared he felt at liberty to attend to his own wants by cooking a supply of provisions for future use.

For two more nights and days was this strange and perilous journey continued, until at daylight of the third day Donald felt that he must be within a few miles of Presque Isle. The most critical moment of his undertaking had now arrived. In spite of the rising sun he must push on, for he was determined to reach the fort if possible before the Indians, and warn Christie of their coming. At the same time he realized that, as they had been able to travel much faster than he in his big canoe, he could not be much if any past their camp of the night just ended. Nor did he dare keep far out in the lake, for fear lest they cut him off from the shore and so hold him at their mercy.

Wearied with his night's work, compelled to keep on, not daring to land, and expecting each moment to hear the exulting yell or crack of a rifle that should announce his discovery, Donald was thus obliged to paddle doggedly forward within a hundred yards of the shore. His suspense was well-nigh unbearable. Every nerve was strung to its utmost tension. In each new indentation of the coast he expected to see the waiting fleet of canoes, and with each fearful backward glance he wondered at not finding them in pursuit.

At length, as he rounded a point, he thought he saw far down the lake, against the blue of the sky and above the sombre forest, a flutter of red. At the same moment be glanced behind him to see if he were still free from pursuit. Alas! He was not. Two canoes, each urged by half a dozen gleaming paddles, were following as swiftly and silently as sharks that had scented blood, and they were not a quarter of a mile away. As their occupants noted that they were discovered they uttered yells of exultation that chilled the poor lad's blood in his veins and caused him to feel faint with a despairing terror.

CHAPTER XXIII
DISCOVERED AND PURSUED BY SAVAGES

It was only for a moment that Donald was overcome by the chill despair that, in presence of an imminent and overwhelming danger, often paralyzes the most resolute. Then it passed as suddenly as it had come. The hot blood surged through his veins, his heart was filled with a fierce joy at the prospect of contest, and, under the vigorous impulse of his stout young arms, the canoe bounded forward as though it were animate and shared his feelings. Perhaps it was all owing to the fact that, having rounded the point, the pursuing savages were momentarily lost to view, and their yells no longer rang in his ears. At any rate, the sudden terror was conquered, as it always is by brave men, though with cowards it stays to the end.

Donald headed straight for the beach, gained it, hastily dragged his canoe behind some bushes, and, seizing only his rifle, plunged into the forest. He reflected that it must be some minutes before his pursuers could strike his trail; and, with that advantage of time, he surely ought to reach the fort in advance of them. So, while he ran at a great speed, he still saved his strength, and by no means did his best. This he reserved for a later emergency.

He had hardly got under way when the spiteful crack of a rifle rang out from the forest directly in front of him. Almost at the same instant he threw up his arms, staggered forward, and fell. As he did so, a painted savage leaped from behind a tree and raised a hand to his mouth to produce the quavering of a triumphant war-whoop. With its first shrill note a second rifle uttered its deadly summons; the exulting Indian leaped high, and fell, pierced by Donald's bullet. Then the latter arose, hastily reloaded, and, with only a contemptuous glance at the dead foe who had been so easily beguiled, sped on his way. There might be other Indians in his path; but if they were all as simple as that fellow, he should not mind them.

The young woodsman had not been harmed nor even grazed by his adversary's bullet, and unexpected as it was, he had been quick-witted enough to put into practice one of Truman Flagg's long-ago lessons. Often, when he was a child, playing in the edge of the woods near Tawtry House, had he flung up his little arms and dropped in that very manner, at the sound of an unexpected shot, fired into the air, from the old scout's rifle. Thus, though he had never before been obliged to resort to it for self-preservation, the action now came to him as naturally as breathing.

Now, as he sped forward, his pace was accelerated by a series of yells that announced the landing, and discovery of his trail by the pursuers whom he had first seen. Then, though an unbroken silence reigned in the pleasant forest glades, he knew that swift runners were on his track and that the time had come for his utmost exertions.

Mile after mile he ran until he had covered a goodly number before his strength began to fail. At length he was panting so that each hissing breath was a stab, and his eyesight grew dim. He plunged, almost headlong, down the precipitous side of a ravine and at its bottom, fell, face downward, into the cool waters of a rippling brook. How deliciously refreshing were the two or three great gulps that he swallowed. How the life-giving fluid thrilled his whole frame! If he could only lie there as long as he chose and drink his fill! But he could not; two magic words rang like bells in his ears, "Edith" and "Christie." For his own life alone he would hardly have prolonged this terrible race with death; but for theirs he must run while he had strength to stand. So, almost as he fell, he was again on his feet and scrambling up the steep opposite side of the ravine.

As he gained its crest, a rattling sound caused him to look back--the foremost of his pursuers was leaping down the farther side. How fresh and powerful he looked--within two minutes he would overtake him. Would he? Edith and Christie! The crack of a rifle, the hiss of a bullet, and the powerful Indian lay quietly beside the little stream as though resting after his long run. Donald had no time for reloading, and flinging away his gun, he again sprang forward.

There was a ringing in his ears; but through it he heard the howls of rage that announced the discovery of the silent one lying by the little stream, and knew that a desire for vengeance would add swiftness to the feet of his pursuers. His own seemed weighted with lead, and he felt that he was crawling; but though he could not realize it he was still running splendidly, and with almost undiminished speed.

As he leaped, crashing through the underbrush, he was mistaken for a deer, and only the quick eye of a hunter who was already raising his rifle for a shot saved him from death at the hands of those whom he would warn of their peril.

"Halt! who comes?" rang out in crisp tones from him who still presented his rifle hesitatingly, as he detected the Indian costume of the advancing runner.

"Friend! The enemy! Oh, Christie!" gasped the fugitive as he staggered into the arms of the young commandant at Fort Presque Isle.

"By Heavens! It is Donald Hester," he cried in terror, "and I came near shooting him for a deer! Thank God! Thank God that my hand was stayed! Why, lad, what is it? You are near dead with running; what danger threatens?"

"Fly, Christie, fly," panted Donald. "The savages are in hot pursuit."

"And leave you, lad? Not while I have breath in my body and a rifle in my hand. Rest a minute and recover your breath while we welcome those who follow you so hotly. Martin, get behind yon tree while I hold this one. Take you the first redskin who appears, and I will deal with the second. That will at least serve to check them while we can reload. Steady! here they come."

It was fortunate indeed for Donald that his friend, seized with a longing for fresh venison, had chosen that morning for a hunt, and, taking a man with him, had entered the forest. They were not yet a half-mile from the fort when they met the exhausted fugitive as described. Now their rifles blazed at other game than deer, and, as Christie had predicted, the pursuit was checked; for only two had followed thus far, though within a mile scores of others were ranging the forest.

The two men instantly reloaded and, without exposing themselves beyond the sheltering tree trunks, waited a full minute without detecting further movement or sound. Then Donald begged them to retreat while there was yet time, and the three set forth for the fort.

As they ran, each of the others passed an arm through one of Donald's, and the woods being open, they were able thus to make good speed. Even as they went, Donald could not repress the one eager inquiry that, in spite of all distractions, was ever uppermost in his thoughts.

[Illustration: Donald and his two companions are pursued by Indians.]

"Edith. Is she safe, Christie?"

"My poor fellow, I know nothing concerning her. I hoped you had news."

"Has Cuyler reached the tort?"

"Yes; and left two days since for Niagara."

"And Edith was not with him?"

"No."

"He knew nothing of her fate?"

"Nothing."

Donald said no more; but his form as supported by the two men became noticeably heavier, as though it had been suddenly deprived of some upbearing and stimulating force.

As the three dashed into the little post, which was only garrisoned by a score of troops, they were none too soon; for, almost at the same moment, a rattling volley and fierce yelling gave notice that the siege of Presque Isle was begun. But the garrison was not taken by surprise, for the shots from the forest had been heard, and half a dozen soldiers had run out to protect the retreat of the fugitives.

Christie's first attention was given to the friend whose coming had not only placed the garrison on guard, but had saved him from being cut off, as he certainly would have been had not his hunting been interrupted. So he led Donald to his own quarters, showed him where to find food and drink, and then left him to recover his strength.

The so-called fort of Presque Isle was but a collection of a dozen low wooden buildings ranged about a parade ground, in which was the single well of the place. It was unprotected by palisades or walls of any kind; but was provided with a citadel in shape of a stout blockhouse that stood at one angle of the fort and was separated by a few yards of open space from the quarters of the commanding officer.

The location of the post was unfortunate, from a military point of view, in that it occupied a small, open flat, commanded on one side by the beach ridge of the lake, and on another by the equally high bank of a stream that entered the lake at a right angle.

The first fire of the enemy, who had fully expected to surprise the place and effect its capture as a mere incident in their pursuit of Cuyler, was delivered from the beach ridge and was harmless. A few minutes later, however, there came a scathing cross-fire from the high creek-bank on the other side. By this, one man who was crossing the parade was killed and several were wounded. A little later tongues of flame appeared on the bark-covered roof of a building, and it was evident that no place of safety existed outside the blockhouse. To this, then, Christie ordered the immediate retreat of his entire force.

Already were the rifles of several picked marksmen blazing from the upper story of this stronghold, and the rest of the garrison, by running close along the sheltering walls of the other buildings, gained in safety the protection of its stout logs.

"Sorry not to give you a little longer breathing spell, old man," said Ensign Christie to Donald, as he entered his own quarters for the last time; "but those chaps out there are so inconsiderate in their shooting that it has become necessary for us to move. So if you will just step over to the castle, we will try to entertain you there, and can at least promise you plenty of occupation."

"All right," replied Donald, "I'm ready, and nearly as fit as ever; but have you any hope of beating them off eventually, Christie? If not, I want to make a break for the woods as soon as it comes dark. I must get back up the lake, for I am not yet prepared to give up the search for my sister Edith."

"Nor shall you, my dear fellow, and I would join you in it with all my heart if it were not for my duty here," replied the other, earnestly. "At present, though, it would be more than folly to attempt an escape from this place, and our only hope is to hold out until Wilkins sends the reinforcements for which I have applied through Cuyler."

"Is there any chance of doing it?"

"There is every chance for us to do our best in trying."

A minute later the two young men had passed into the blockhouse, its heavy oaken door was slammed and barred behind them, and the defence of the little wilderness stronghold was begun.

CHAPTER XXIV
CHRISTIE'S BRAVE DEFENCE OF HIS POST

Twenty men, with scanty supplies of everything, shut up in a tiny castle of logs, and fighting against two hundred, who were well armed, well provisioned, and protected by natural earthworks, not over forty yards distant. Donald's heart grew heavy as he realized the situation; but with Christie's cheery voice in his ears he could do naught save follow so brave an example and set to work with a will. There was plenty to be done in that hot little enclosure, already filling with smoke, and only lighted by narrow loop-holes pierced in the thick walls. The fire of the enemy was chiefly directed at these, which rendered the task of watching from them most dangerous. Still, it must be done, for many of the Indians were brave enough to dash across the open with blazing firebrands in hand, and these must be stopped at all costs. Half a dozen were killed in this attempt before it was abandoned, and the efforts to set the blockhouse on fire were continued by another and most ingenious device.

This was the throw-stick, or fire-bow, which they soon began to work with serious effect from behind their breastworks, which they had strengthened by rolling logs to the top of the banks. The fire-bow was a stout bar of ash, hickory, or other pliant wood, one end of which was firmly set in the earth. In the other was hollowed a shallow cavity, and just beneath was attached a stout thong, by which the bow could be drawn back. A ball of tow, or other inflammable material, wound about a small stone to give it weight, was saturated with pitch. The upper end of the bow was drawn back, a fire ball placed in the cavity and lighted, the thong released, and the blazing missile projected with the force and accuracy of an arrow against the devoted building.

Again and again its walls caught fire, but each blaze was extinguished by the activity of the garrison as soon as discovered.

Fire-arrows, shot into the air, fell on the dry shingles of the roof, and hardly a minute passed that a tiny blaze did not spring from one part or another of it. The roof could be gained from the interior, through an opening protected on two sides by a barricade of plank, and here Donald was stationed, at his own request.

From this elevated position he soon discovered a new danger, and one that he had never before heard of in Indian warfare. He could see quantities of earth and stones being thrown out behind one of the breastworks, and became convinced that the enemy were excavating a subterranean passage, or mine, toward the blockhouse. So well did the young soldier realize the terrible menace of this new danger, against which no defence could be made, that he dared not announce it to the troops for fear of disheartening them. So, deserting his post for a moment, he hastened to report it in person to Christie.

Ere the latter had time to consider this peril, another equally grave and more imminent confronted him. The water barrels were nearly empty, and the roof was again on fire. Donald rushed back to his post, while Christie ordered two men to follow him to the lower story. He knew that without water all hope of resistance must quickly disappear. Certain death awaited him who should attempt to reach the well in the parade ground. There was no other.

"So," said Christie, with a calm cheerfulness, "we must needs dig one nearer at hand." With this, he and his two men set to work tearing up the floor of the lower story, and, seizing a spade, the commander himself began flinging out the earth beneath it.

Inspired by this example, his men worked with a will at this cheerless task, and in spite of darkness, heat, thirst, and the suffocating atmosphere, never was a well sunk more quickly. At the same time it was not half completed when so serious a fire broke out on the roof that the entire remaining stock of water was exhausted in extinguishing it.

An hour later the roof was again in a blaze; but Donald caused himself to be lowered by a rope, and amid a shower of bullets tore away the flaming shingles with his bare hands. Thus was the danger once more averted.

By this time the day was well spent. Several of the garrison had been killed, and a number were wounded. These last called piteously for water, and gazed with longing eyes at the limitless expanse of the lake, so near at hand and yet so hopelessly remote. By sunset the well-diggers were in moist earth, before nine o'clock the wounded were eagerly quaffing a muddy liquid that gave them new life, and by midnight two feet of water stood in the well.

During the night, although the enemy's fire was slackened, it never entirely ceased. Balls of blazing pitch were discharged at frequent intervals, and no moment of rest was allowed the weary garrison. At daybreak, exulting cries from the rear, and a ruddy glow, announced some new cause for anxiety. In a few minutes the worst was known. The underground approach had been advanced as far as Christie's quarters, which were immediately set on fire. Only a narrow space separated this building from the blockhouse, and with the fierce blaze of its pine logs the stifling heat in the latter became almost unsupportable. It seemed to the men that the time to yield had come; but their commander was not yet ready to acknowledge the situation as hopeless. Even when the scorched and smoking walls of their prison house burst into flame, he only bade them work the harder, and inspired them by his own heroism. Thanks to the new well, they succeeded in holding the flames in check until the blazing building that had threatened them finally sank into a mass of glowing embers, and their little fortress still stood intact.

With the reaction following this supreme effort, many of the men again gave way to despair. All were sickened by the great heat, the stifling smoke, and the exhaustion of twenty-four hours of continuous fighting. Donald held to his strength better than any, because from his perilous position on the roof he could at least breathe pure air; while Christie, who fought beside his men, was so upheld by his indomitable will that he would not acknowledge fatigue.

So the defence was maintained, until the second day of incessant toil, fighting, and hoping against hope for relief, dragged out its weary length, and darkness once more brooded over Presque Isle. From behind the breastworks rifles flashed incessantly until midnight, when the firing ceased, and from out of the darkness a voice hailed the fort in English.

"What is wanted?" demanded Christie.

"You are called upon to surrender," answered the voice, "since further resistance is useless."

"And if I refuse?"

"Then you will shortly be blown into eternity. Your fort is undermined, and a great store of powder is already in position to blow it up. If you surrender, your lives shall be spared."

"Ask them to wait until morning for your answer," suggested Donald, in a low tone. "I have a particular reason for the request."

Christie agreed to this, and the proposition was submitted.

There was a long pause, and an evident discussion, before the voice answered:--

"The beggars will only grant that request on one condition."

"Name it."

"It is that neither you nor those under your command shall make any attempt to escape during the time of truce."

"Am I under your command, Christie?" asked Donald.

"Certainly not," was the answer.

"All right. I only wanted to be sure that the condition wouldn't bind me."

"Well," cried the voice, impatiently, "do you agree?"

"I agree," replied Christie, "and by sunrise will have ready my final answer."

In the profound and grateful quiet that followed the cessation of firing, most of the exhausted garrison flung themselves down where they stood, and were instantly buried in slumber. Donald and Christie sought food, and while they ate discussed the situation.

"You have splendidly defended your post, Christie, but you have come to the end of your resources," said the former. "You could not hold out for another day, even if what that fellow said about the mine should prove false."

"No, I suppose not," replied the young commander, sadly. "My poor lads are nearly used up."

"Then you will surrender?"

"I suppose so."

"In that case, they will probably spare your lives, at least until they get you to the Indian villages near Detroit."

"They may do so."

"But you will be prisoners, and that is what I cannot afford to become. I must retain my freedom, if it lies within my power to do so, until I have found Edith, or discovered her fate."

"What do you propose to do?" inquired Christie, starting from his despondent attitude.

"I mean to leave this place within an hour and take to the woods."

"But--"

"There are no buts, my dear fellow. I am determined to make the attempt. You have acknowledged that I am not under your command, and so am not held by the condition just imposed. I hate to leave you, and would a thousand times rather stand by you and share your fate, whatever it may be; but my duty seems to lie so plainly in another direction that I must go."

"You are right, Hester," assented Christie, sadly, "and with all my heart do I wish I were free to share your mission. There is no peril, no hardship, that I would not gladly face in the cause for which you are enlisted. I tremble, though, for your safety, and cannot believe that you will escape without detection from the savages who encircle us."

"I can try," answered Donald, "and the cause is certainly worthy of the effort."

So it was settled, and soon afterward the two young men, whose friendship had become like the love of brothers, stood by the partially opened door of the blockhouse. The night was of inky blackness, and the silence was profound. Only a dull glow still lighted faintly the smouldering ruins of the commandant's quarters. Donald held a rifle, and bore with him a stout knife, a small supply of ammunition, and a little store of food. No word accompanied the parting. There was but a long, firm hand clasp, and then one was gone as noiselessly as a fleeting shadow, while the other remained to meet his unknown fate.

CHAPTER XXV
DONALD FIRES THE MINE AND SAVES THE BLOCKHOUSE

Knowing the savage nature as well as he did, Donald believed that his well-loved friend, as well as every one of the gallant fellows under his command, would be put to death in case they surrendered; or, if they were spared for the time being, it would only be for torture in the Indian villages. He was determined, therefore, to make an effort to save them; but his half-formed plan was of such a perilous nature that he dared not confide it to Christie, for he knew that the latter would never consent to its being undertaken. Once outside the blockhouse, however, and lost to sight in the darkness, he was free to act as he pleased.

After going a few steps he paused to listen, but no sound save that of night-birds and the lapping of little waves on the lake shore came to his ears. The silence was profound, and assured him that even the savages, wearied with long fighting, were snatching a few hours of sleep. On either side of him lay the still smoking ruins of the post, for of all its buildings, the stronghold of logs alone remained standing.

From these charred heaps, fitful flames, fanned into life by the soft night breeze, sprang up every now and then, casting fantastic bits of light and shadow over the scene of desolation.

Reassured by the silence, the young soldier swiftly crossed the open space beyond which lay the forest, and skirted the latter to the lake shore. There he hid his rifle and his supplies in the hollow of a tree, so that he might have greater freedom of action. Then he worked his way cautiously toward the rude breastworks facing the blockhouse. A small fire of driftwood burned dimly behind these, and about it sat several blanketed figures. In no other direction was there a sign of wakefulness.

Donald was now crawling on hands and knees. Suddenly he encountered a figure lying prone in his path, and had touched it before aware of its proximity. Instantly he, too, lay flat on the ground, and, with heavy breathing, so feigned sleep that the aroused savage was deceived into believing the form beside him to be that of some restless comrade. So he turned over with a grunt, and again dozed into unconsciousness.

After a few minutes Donald ventured to move, and then to pursue his way with a greater caution than before. Now he passed other sleeping forms, and even stepped over one whom he could not otherwise avoid. Finally, after more than an hour of intense anxiety and stealthy movement, only advancing by inches, and with frequent motionless pauses, he discovered the place of which he was in search. It was the mouth of the mine that the Indians had spent two days and nights in excavating. As he had conjectured, it lay very near the little fire beside which sat the drowsy guard, and not until he was well within its profound shadow did he venture to draw a full breath.

At War with Pontiac

The passage was very low, but of sufficient width to allow two persons to pass each other, and after penetrating it a short distance he found that it took a turn to the left. At this angle he was perplexed by coming into contact with fragments of charred wood. Wondering for what purpose these had been brought there, he still moved forward, determined to discover whether or not the statement concerning a store of powder beneath the blockhouse was true. All at once his outstretched hands came into contact with something that barred his further progress. It was hard, smooth, and round. There were other similar objects above, below, and on both sides of it. They were powder kegs, five in all, and of a size that should contain twenty pounds. One hundred pounds of powder! Enough to lift the little fortress from its foundations and scatter its timbers far and wide. The savages had made no empty boast, and, unless he could save his recent companions, their fate was surely sealed.

What could he do? Time was precious, for daylight could not be far off. Beyond this point he had formed no plan. He had hoped to find both the tunnel and its contents but an ingenious fiction to frighten Christie into a surrender. Now it was a startling and overwhelming truth. He could not remove the powder by the way he had come. In fact, he doubted if he could effect his own escape that way, so thickly were the sleeping savages dispersed about the entrance to the tunnel. In this predicament, and with the intensity of his thinking, great beads of perspiration started to his forehead, and he clenched his hands until they ached.

The mine was all ready for firing. He knew this by discovering that one of the powder kegs was open, and by finding the end of a rudely made fuse buried in its contents. Who had taught the Indians this diabolical trick of warfare? Never before had they been known to prepare a mine. They must have been instructed by some white man, and one possessed of military knowledge. All at once Donald recalled the voice that had demanded the surrender of the blockhouse. Certainly, no Indian ever spoke English like that. Had there not been a familiar ring to the tones? It seemed so now, though he had been too intent on other thoughts to notice it at the time. Still he was not sure, the impression was too slight.

All these things flashed through Donald's mind in a moment, while his hands were feeling out the exact condition of the mine. How long was that fuse? He traced it backward as its evil length stretched along the bottom of the tunnel. It led to the angle, and there he again encountered the fragments of burned wood. At one side the tunnel widened, and here its wall was entirely composed of this material. Where could it have come from? It was freshly charred. The Indians would never have brought it there and piled it in that confusion. It must have fallen from above! There must be an opening! If there only was, he would know just what to do. There would be no difficulty then about forming a plan.

With eager haste Donald began pulling away the burned ends of timbers and logs. He had hardly begun before the whole mass gave way, and slid down on him. Fortunately, there was not much of it, and, though he was nearly smothered by dust and ashes, he quickly scrambled from the debris, and listened with loudly beating heart. He realized that he had found an opening to the surface, and was wildly exultant over the discovery, but could hardly believe that the noise of the sliding material, which had sounded to him like an avalanche, should not have aroused the savages. So, for some minutes, he listened, and then, reassured by the continued silence, ventured to climb up to the open air. He had but a few feet to go, and once at the surface instantly recognized his surroundings. He was beside the ruins of Christie's quarters, and just beyond rose the black mass of the blockhouse, in which he had recently suffered so much.

But that glow in the east, against which it was outlined so distinctly! It could not be that the night was already gone and daylight near at hand. Yes, it was, though; and, realizing that his working time was now limited to minutes, Donald slid back into the tunnel, and began to carry the powder kegs, one at a time, toward its outer end, placing them as near the entrance as he dared venture. He was forced to work slowly in that confined space, as well as with the utmost caution; for, by the rapidly increasing light, he caught occasional glimpses of dusky forms passing and repassing the entrance, showing that the enemy was already astir. He expected each time that he returned from the further end of the mine to be confronted by some burly savage, and became so nervous at the prospect that the utmost exercise of his will power was required to enable him to complete his task. At length it was finished. All the kegs were removed to their new position and piled about the one whose open head admitted the fuse. The other end of this reached half way to the new place of exit.

Almost breathless with nervous excitement, he knelt beside the farther end of the fuse, and with trembling hands attempted to ignite it by a spark struck from flint and steel. Again and again the spark flew aside, but at length there came a slight flash and a spluttering flame.

Heavens! How fast that roughly made fuse burned! Almost like an open train of powder. Donald had hardly thought of his own danger; but a single glance at that hissing line of fire caused him to spring to his place of exit. He scrambled through it, and darted at full speed across the open toward the forest, heedless of everything save a desire to place as great a distance as possible between himself and the awful fire fiend about to leap forth.

As he reached the edge of the woods and turned to look, the explosion came. He saw a sheet of vivid flame, that dimmed the brightness of the rising sun, leaping in air. At the same instant, as though it had been a thunderbolt and hurled at him, he was struck senseless by a crashing blow on the head, delivered from behind.

The four or five crouching figures that had been grimly watching Donald's approach, and sprang up to receive him as he turned to look back, were for a moment petrified with fright at the suddenness and violence of the shock. Then, moved by a common impulse, and without a word being spoken, they lifted their unconscious captive, ran with him to the lake shore, bundled him into a canoe, and pushed off.

Upon the Indians behind the breastwork, where the full force of the explosion was felt, the effect was so disastrous that the panic-stricken survivors rushed madly for their canoes. Many of these were damaged, and some crushed beyond repair, by the rain of logs, stones, and other missiles hurled from the dense smoke-cloud that was slowly drifting to leeward in fleecy folds.

Although the blockhouse was violently shaken, it remained standing, and, after a moment of consternation, its garrison rushed out to hasten the flight of their terrified foes. A few ran to the breastwork on the lake shore, and gazed wonderingly at the smoking hole from which the torrent of flame had burst. The rest, headed by Christie, charged upon the Indians behind the creek hank, who, although preparing for flight, were not quite so bereft of their senses as those who had felt the full shock of the upheaval. Some of them even turned on the whites, who rushed so recklessly among them; so that for a minute a fierce hand-to-hand fight raged on the narrow strand, and even among the crowded canoes in the water. In the confusion of this melee Christie became separated from his men, and ere he realized the full peril of his position received several knife wounds in quick succession. Staggering under these, he fell, was instantly dragged into a canoe, and borne away.

It was only after the last of the canoes had made good its escape, leaving many dead savages behind, that the little force of breathless but exulting soldiers discovered their leader to be missing. In vain did they search for him. In vain did they run along the shore, firing ineffectual shots at the departing fleet. He was not to be found, nor had they any knowledge of his fate.

So their jubilation over this wonderful deliverance and victory was turned into sorrow, and it was with heavy hearts that, abandoning the little fortress, they set forth on a retreat towards the Niagara.

CHAPTER XXVI
FRIENDS IN CAPTIVITY

Not until the panic-stricken savages had put many miles of water between them and the scene of their recent discomfiture did they venture to land and establish a camp in which to attend to their wounded, repair damaged canoes, and recover as far as possible from the disaster of the morning. Among the first craft to make a landing was that in which Donald Hester, after slowly recovering consciousness, had lain for several hours, nearly blinded with a headache, so intense that a band of fire seemed to encircle his throbbing temples, vaguely wondering what had happened and where he was. On reaching the shore, the other occupants of the canoe disappeared without paying any attention to him; and, being thus left to his own devices, he proceeded to quench his feverish thirst as well as bathe his aching head. He wondered at finding blood clotted in his hair, and, dimly recalling the explosion, fancied that in some way he must have been among its victims. While he was thus engaged, other canoes were arriving and being drawn up on the beach. Beyond them fires were lighted, and already savory odors of cooking reminded him how very faint he was from hunger. While considering how he should procure some of the food that seemed so abundant, his gaze was suddenly arrested by the appearance of a white man, who was stepping feebly from one of the latest-arrived canoes. For a moment Donald could hardly believe his own eyes. Then he strode hastily forward with outstretched hand.

"Christie, my dear fellow! Is it possible?"

"Donald! How came you here?" exclaimed the new arrival, his drawn face lighting with the recognition of a dear friend amid so many enemies.

"But you are wounded!" they both cried at once.

"A mere nothing," said Donald.

"Only a few scratches," answered Christie, in a careless tone.

Each insisted on bathing and binding up, as well as circumstances would admit, the hurts of the other, for which purpose they tore strips from Christie's shirt. Donald was relieved to find that the knife-cuts from which his friend was bleeding were only flesh wounds, and not at all dangerous; while the latter was equally pleased to discover that the ugly gash on Donald's head looked much more serious than it really was.

Their surgical operations ended, the two sought some place where they might rest, and learn from each other the causes of the captivity that brought about such an unexpected meeting. They seemed to be unguarded and left entirely to their own devices, but the moment they attempted to go beyond the noisy limits of the camp they were confronted by a rifle-bearing young warrior who sternly motioned them back. Being thus repulsed several times, they were finally compelled to sit under a tree, well within the confines of the camp and in view of all its busy occupants. Here Christie learned of Donald's adventures since their midnight parting, and, while applauding his bravery, chided him for engaging in so dangerous an undertaking.

"If it had only been wholly successful, and left you at liberty," said Donald, "I should feel amply repaid."

"And so it would have done, but for my own carelessness," replied Christie, who thereupon gave an account of the explosion, its effect on the savages, and the manner in which he had fallen into their hands, while his men escaped. "I can't understand that mine business, though," he said, in conclusion, "for I had no idea Indians were up to such things."

"Do you recall the capital English of the person who demanded your surrender last night?" asked Donald.

"Certainly."

"Did the voice sound at all familiar?"

"I can't say that it did. Why?"

"It was that of an Englishman, though?"

"I believe so. And of course it was he who devised the plan of the mine. He must have been some renegade British soldier. The scoundrel! Would that I had him in my power for just five minutes! He must have met his just deserts, though, and fallen a victim to his own diabolical trap, thanks to you, for, besides ourselves, there is certainly no white man in this camp."

"If that is the case, and my own surmise is a true one, I don't know whether I am most glad or sorry," said Donald.

"What do you mean? What is your surmise?" inquired Christie, curiously.

"Do you remember that I mentioned seeing a certain bath-tub in one of the canoes that brought this war-party?"

"Bullen's? Of course I do. But you can't for an instant imagine that he had a hand in this outrage?"

"Well, you undoubtedly know the paymaster better than I, but I must confess that I should like to meet him, and hear his own account of his movements during the past ten days or so."

"That you are not likely to do, at least not for some time to come, if ever; and in the meantime I wish you could dismiss from your mind every shadow of such a terrible suspicion against a brother officer," said Christie, gravely.

"All right, my dear fellow, I will try to do so out of admiration for your loyalty to our cloth, if for no other reason. Now, to change the subject, what do you suppose is going on over there?"

"I have been wondering," replied Christie, "and at the same time admiring the barbaric gorgeousness of that central figure. He is certainly the most terrific dandy in savage style that ever I laid eyes on. Seems to be in some sort of a mess with his fellow-heathen, too, judging from his expression and surroundings. It looks like some sort of forest court-martial: and, by Jove! I believe it is one."

The scene thus referred to was that of a circle of grave warriors seated about a small fire, and listening to the harangue of one who stood in an open space reserved for him at one side. Beyond the circle were gathered the younger men and such squaws as were free from culinary duties. The speaker was, as Christie had remarked, an Indian dandy of the most extreme type, although short in stature as compared with the long-limbed warriors surrounding him. His head was surmounted by a gaudily colored plume of feathers held in place by a glittering band or tiara that encircled his brows. Secured about his waist by a broad belt of rattlesnake skin, but falling back from the upper part of his body, was a fine white blanket edged with fur and so elaborately embroidered with beads and quills that the original fabric was almost concealed. His feet and ankles were protected by moccasins of fawn skin, also beautifully embroidered. But the triumph of forest art, as displayed on his person, lay in the wonderful painting of his entire body, which was covered with intricate designs in the most vivid colors on a background of black, and the prismatic effect was so bewilderingly gorgeous, that, as Christie said to Donald, "it was enough to mortify a rainbow."

In spite of his paint and feathers the individual thus lavishly decorated did not seem happy. In fact, he appeared miserably nervous and apprehensive; or, as Christie remarked, as though he had been condemned to exchange his gaudiness for something more modest, like the plumage of a peacock, for instance. "Isn't he lovely, though?" continued the young officer. "Now I know, what I should never otherwise have suspected, that the savage mind is capable of an artistic expression more sublime than anything yet conceived by civilization."

"Yes," replied Donald, absently, "but there are several things about the fellow that I don't understand. To begin with, he is talking to those other chaps through an interpreter. Then he does not gesticulate, while most Indian orators depend more upon signs than words for effect. He stands with his toes turned out, and his ears are not cut. In fact, I don't believe he is any more an Indian than I am."

"What do you think he is?" inquired Christie, apprehensively.

"I don't know what he is; but I believe him to be an--a Frenchman."

"Oh!" said the other, in a relieved tone. "Do you really? I--Hello? what's that? Bullen's tub! By Jove!"

One of the older chiefs had been talking for a few moments, and now, evidently by his command, two young men brought the famous bath-tub into the circle and set it down close beside the dandy. Another presented a dish of water. The gorgeous individual shuddered as he took it, like one showing the first symptoms of hydrophobia. He looked imploringly about him, said something which was answered by an angry exclamation to the effect that the order just given must be obeyed.

The man stooped, took something from a compartment in the tub, with trembling hand, apparently dropped it into the vessel of water, and lifted the latter into plain view. In a breathless silence all eyes were turned toward it. For a moment the gorgeous one held it aloft, and then, as no result followed his manipulation, he dropped it with a sort of a groan, and gazed about him with the tearfulness of a hunted animal.

A murmur of discontent arose from the savage throng surrounding him. Donald glanced at Christie, whose face had grown deadly pale, but said nothing. Both young men had risen in their excitement, and now stood watching the strange scene with eager interest.

Now the elderly warrior picked up a stone and handed it to the dandy with an expressive gesture. Instead of obeying he shook his head despairingly, and an ominous growl came from the assemblage. Again Donald looked at Christie, whose face was now tense and drawn, as though he were suffering mental anguish.

Amid a deadly silence the warrior again advanced, and handed the man a smooth piece of bark, at the same time making certain motions that seemed to be clearly understood. The unfortunate dandy took the bark and held it irresolutely for a moment, while his gaze roved wildly over the assembly. All at once it rested on the two white men, whose presence he seemed to note for the first time. With a loud cry he dropped the bark and started to run in their direction.

In an instant he was seized, and with yells of rage the throng of savages rushed toward him. Eager hands tore away the nodding plume of feathers, the embroidered robe, and whatever else they could clutch, until only his coat of paint remained. Then, as the warriors stepped aside, the squaws, armed with sticks and clubs, fell upon him like so many furies, beating him unmercifully. He howled, danced, fought, ran this way and that, and, finally, breaking from his tormentors, fled to where the two young men were standing.

"Save me!" he cried. "Christie! Hester! save me!"

"By Heavens! It is Bullen!" gasped Christie.

"So I thought some time ago," said Donald.

As the fugitive reached them, he sprang behind Donald, crying,--

"The mark on your arm, Hester! Show it to them! Nothing else will save us!"

With these words he clutched at the sleeve of Donald's hunting-shirt with such energy it was torn from the shoulder, and the tattooed token was fully displayed. At sight of it the foremost of the mob, which had been intent on capturing the trembling figure, now crouched behind Donald, halted as though in obedience to an imperious order. Then they crowded forward for a closer examination of the talismanic mark, staring at it with expressions of awe and wonder.

CHAPTER XXVII
HOW THE PAYMASTER NAVIGATED LAKE ERIE IN A TUB

As already stated, Donald was ignorant of the meaning of the mark tattooed on his arm, but with this manifestation of its power he could not longer doubt that, to Indian eyes at least, its significance was of great importance. This was the third time that it had afforded him material aid in times of critical danger, though Bullen had witnessed its effect but once, and Christie never until the present moment. Moreover, as the latter had not learned until now that his friend bore such a mark, his amazement at the paymaster's appearance was divided with curiosity concerning it. That it was a powerful talisman was proved by the evidence; for not only had the furious squaws who were belaboring poor Bullen slunk away when it was extended protectingly above him, but the warriors now gazing at it were evidently animated only by a respectful curiosity. As Christie also looked at the magic emblem, he saw the outline of an animal, that might be meant for a bear, encircled by an oval formed of two serpents. Above the whole was a tiny triangle, enclosing the rude semblance of an eye.

Several of the Indians surrounding Donald pointed to figures on their own arms, similar to that of the animal on his, but without the remainder of the device. These gravely shook hands with him, and then walked away. Then came the one who had acted as Bullen's interpreter, and proudly displayed on his arm a tattooed mark identical with that borne by Donald, save that the surmounting eye was not enclosed. This man did not offer to shake hands; but, folding his arms in a peculiar manner, as though to indicate the oval of serpents, bowed and asked, in broken French: "What will my brother of the magic circle have? It is his to command, and mine to obey."

"I will have," replied the young man, quickly adapting his tone to the occasion, "food for myself and my friend. Then I would be left for a season, that I may question this white man, who, painted like a son of the forest, yet seeks my protection. Also, if my brother of the Metai is so inclined, I would learn something of the charge against him."

"It shall be done as my brother desires," answered the other. "As to the charge against this white man, it must also be told, for all things may be learned by the Metai. Know, then, that he came to us as a great medicine man, who wished to become Indian. He performed marvellous deeds, and won our confidence. He offered to show us how we might safely capture the fort of the log house. He placed powder so as to destroy it. Then, in the night, when all was ready, he moved the powder by his magic. Without going near the place where it was he made it to explode, so that it killed many of our young men, and turned to water the hearts of others. For this wickedness the Great Spirit took from him his medicine, so that he can no longer do the things he once did, as was shown in the tests but now. Therefore is he become a dog, and must die as a dog when my brother shall be finished with him."

"It is well," replied Donald, gravely, "and later I will speak further concerning this matter with my brother of the Metai, and with the chiefs."

With another profound bow the interpreter retired, while the squaws brought an abundance of cooked meat and parched corn, which they set before the famished white men. One of them also brought bandages, and a healing salve for the dressing of Donald's wound; but by signs he intimated that she must first attend to Christie's hurts, which she did.

Then they were left to themselves, and fell ravenously upon the food; but when Christie saw that Bullen was about to eat with them, he drew back, and said sternly: "Hester, I doubt if it is becoming for officers loyal to His Majesty's service to break bread with one who is, to say the least, under a grave suspicion of treachery."

"Do you mean that I am thus suspected?" demanded the paymaster.

"I do, Mr. Bullen," replied Christie.

"But I can easily explain everything. You see--"

"Were you not with the enemy during the attack on Fort Presque Isle?"

"Yes; but--"

"Did you not teach him to throw up breastworks and open a mine?"

"I did; but--"

"Was it not you who demanded the surrender of the post?"

"It was; but as--"

"That will do, sir. Your admissions are sufficient to debar you from our company. Hester, if this man insists upon eating now, we must let him eat alone."

"For Heaven's sake, gentlemen!" cried the little man, with an agonized expression on his painted face. "Do not condemn me without a hearing. I can explain everything to your satisfaction, indeed I can."

"It seems to me that you are a little hasty in your conclusions, Christie," said Donald. "It is certainly unfair to condemn a man without hearing what he has to say, and I for one am too hungry to listen to Mr. Bullen's explanations before eating. So let us fall to and dispose of the more pressing matter before we consider the more important."

Although Christie accepted this advice, he did so with a bad grace, for he was feeling very keenly the loss of his post; and the meal was eaten in an embarrassing silence. When it was finished, they rid themselves of its debris by simply removing to another place, where, though many eyes watched them curiously from all parts of the camp, they were allowed to converse unmolested.

"Now, Mr. Bullen," said Donald, who was forced to take the lead by Christie's stiff silence, "we shall be pleased to listen to your story, and especially glad to have you explain away the suspicions which, you must confess, we have grounds for entertaining."

"Yes," replied the little paymaster, whose present humbleness was in striking contrast to his former pomposity, "I can understand how, from your point of view, my recent course of action may be open to misconception. I hope, however, to prove to you very quickly that, while I may have made mistakes and played the part of a fool, I have acted with the most honorable intentions, as well as with a sincere desire to advance the cause to which I am pledged. You need not fear that I shall omit any detail, nor fail to state the exact facts of the case, for I realize only too clearly how absolutely my reputation rests in the hands of you two. I also believe that my very life depends on Hester's influence with yonder savages, and the extent to which he is willing to exert it. Therefore, with your permission, I will begin my story at the moment when, as I was taking my accustomed evening bath on Pelee Point some ten days ago, there came a sound of distant firing that caused you, Hester, to seize your gun and disappear without a word. I must say that at the time I felt rather sore over your desertion, nor can I understand now how it is that I meet you so far from those whom I thought you were most anxious to discover and protect."

"Do you mean," demanded Donald, excitedly, "that you know what became of my sister Edith and her companion?"

"I do, for I not only spent two days in their company about a week ago, but it is owing to Miss Hester, your sister, that I find myself in this present predicament."

"How? Where? Are they safe?" demanded both listeners.

"I believe them to be comparatively safe," replied Bullen, "but if you will permit me to continue my story in my own way, you can judge for yourselves."

"Very well! only get on quickly," urged Christie, who was now as eagerly interested as he had been indifferent but a moment before.

"As I was saying," continued the paymaster, "Hester had hardly disappeared when both myself and my man were seized by the Indians of our crew, and for a moment I thought they were about to put us to death. Then they hit on another plan with regard to me, which was to set me adrift, naked as I was, in my tub. What they did with poor Tummas I have no knowledge."

"Set you adrift in your tub?" repeated Donald, incredulously.

"Yes. You know I always claimed that it was a capital life preserver, though I must admit that I would have chosen to test its sea-going qualities on a body of water somewhat smaller than Lake Erie. However, as I had no choice in the matter, I was set adrift, as I say. Fortunately for me the sea was smooth, for an off-shore breeze soon carried me beyond reach and sight of land, where I must quickly have been swamped had there been any waves moving. After awhile I became so thoroughly chilled and benumbed that I thought I should perish with the cold, as indeed I should, had I not bethought me of the canvas hood on the back of my tub. This, after infinite labor, and the most careful balancing to prevent an upset, I finally managed to obtain. Wrapped in it, I made out to exist through that fearful night, which seemed as though it would never end.

"In the morning I was out of sight of land, though soon after sunrise I detected a speck lying in the direction I was taking, that afterwards proved to be a small island. A breeze sprang up with the sun, and though it drove me along more rapidly, it also sent little waves slopping over the sides of my tub, so that I was obliged to bail pretty constantly with a sponge. At the same time I was broiled and frizzled by the blaze of the sun on my bare body. To remedy this, I bit away some of the stitches in the bottom of my canvas bag, until I made an opening through which I could thrust my head. I completed the garment thus formed by opening holes in the sides for my arms. Upon my unprotected head, which, as you see, is inclined to be bald, the sun beat with such fury that I feared my brain would be affected, until I conceived the happy thought of tying on a wet sponge.

"By the time I was thus equipped, it was nearly noon, and the island I had been approaching all the morning was close at hand. I saw, however, that I was in danger of drifting past without touching it, and to avert this evil I began to paddle with my hands. In order to preserve the equilibrium of the tub under these efforts I was obliged to paddle it back foremost. Thus I was completely hidden from the shore, nor could I see it save at a distance on either side.

"At length, when I was about used up by this unaccustomed exertion, my craft touched bottom, and I joyfully stepped out in water not over my knees. To my dismay, I was immediately seized by a couple of savages, who had evidently been waiting for me, and found that I had escaped from one enemy only to fall into the hands of another. The feeling thus experienced was, however, as nothing compared with what I underwent when I saw standing but a short distance away three ladies, who were regarding me with curiosity and amazement. Imagine, if you can, my mingled horror and pleasure at recognizing in two of them the very persons whom you and I, Hester, had been so anxious to overtake."

"Not my sister!" cried Donald.

"Yes, your sister, Miss Edith, and Madam Rothsay. I don't think they recognized me at first, for when I tried to make the best of the situation by speaking and expressing my happiness at thus meeting them, Miss Edith gave a sort of a gasp and cried: 'Why, aunty! I do believe it is Mr. Bullen!' She seemed so distressed, that I hastened not only to assure her of my identity, but that with the exception of a few blisters I was quite well. I also attempted to divert her mind by praising the wonderful sea-going qualities of my tub; but all at once she--"

"Oh, Bullen! Bullen! oh Lord! I imagine the tableau!" roared Donald, shouting with uncontrollable laughter at the scene thus presented to his imagination. Even Christie smiled. The startled Indians regarded the white men with wonder, and the little paymaster gazed at Donald with mute indignation.

CHAPTER XXVIII
THE PAYMASTER IN WAR-PAINT AND FEATHERS

"That is just what Miss Edith did," remarked Bullen, in a grieved tone, when Donald's outburst of mirth had somewhat subsided.

"What?"

"Laughed. And when I tried to convince her that my unfortunate predicament was not a subject for merriment, she only laughed the more, until finally she ran away and disappeared in the forest, with which most of the island was covered."

"Well, I don't blame her," said Donald. "Why, man, the spectacle must have been enough to make a graven image chuckle. Didn't Madam Rothsay laugh, too?"

"Certainly not. She only coughed and smiled and apologized in the sweetest manner for having accidentally been a witness to my arrival; hoped they would have the pleasure of seeing me later after I had recovered from the effects of my voyage, and all that sort of thing. Behaved in the most lady-like manner, by Jove."

"And the third lady? By the way, who was she?"

"Oh, she was only an Indian girl; but a stunner, for all that. She may have laughed, but I didn't notice; for she ran after Miss Edith. I found out about her afterwards. She is Pontiac's daughter, and her name is Ah-mo, which means the bee or the sweet one. She was educated in the convent at Montreal and went into society there. Refused a French count, I believe, and all that sort of thing. Don't you remember the fellows at Niagara were talking of her? As near as I could make out, she had been sent by her father to look after the ladies at the time of the attack on Cuyler's party, and was acting the part of hostess when I met them, or something of that kind."

"Ah-mo," repeated Donald, meditatively, and smiling as though the name recalled a pleasant vision. "Well, what became of you after that?"

"Oh! when they saw that I was a friend of the ladies, those Indian chaps behaved very decently; took me to their camp, gave me something to eat, and fixed me up as well as they knew how. Of course I was obliged to do the best I could with what they had to offer, and as paint constituted the principal part of their costume I was obliged to make use of it. They all took a hand at decorating me, and I must say that I think the of my appearance as an Ottawa warrior was rather neat."

"Extremely so," admitted Donald.

"That white blanket I borrowed from Miss Pontiac," continued the little paymaster, "and the moccasins I got from her brother. Of course there wasn't such a thing as a wig to be had, and so I made a liberal use of feathers in its place. The best part of the day was spent in getting me into shape, and when I called on the ladies in the evening I vow they didn't recognize me. Took me for a sure-enough Indian, and thinking I didn't understand English, I suppose, passed remarks on my appearance.

"'Isn't he a guy?' said Miss Edith.

"'Not at all,' replied Madam Rothsay; 'he is by far the best-looking Indian I have seen, and I shouldn't be surprised if he were Pontiac himself.'"

Here Donald winked at Christie.

"When I thanked her for the compliment," continued the paymaster, "and they recognized my voice, I thought that Miss Edith would have a fit, she laughed so immoderately. In fact, she did nothing but laugh whenever she caught sight of me until an event occurred that gave her something more serious to think about. It struck me as being pretty rough on a man who was trying to make the most of his opportunity to win her good graces."

"What happened to divert her from the absurdity of your masquerade?" inquired Christie.

"Nothing more nor less than news of the proposed attack on you," replied Bullen. "During the second day of my stay on the island, the war-party destined for Presque Isle came along and camped there for a few hours. I had been amusing myself and establishing a reputation as medicine man among the few Indians stationed there, by rehearsing some of my old tricks, and when this new gang appeared, nothing would do but an exhibition for their benefit. They were so impressed with my power over the fire-demon, that they invited me to join them. They promised me all sorts of honors if I would comply, and threatened to test my powers by subjecting me to torture by fire in case I refused. I had no idea at that time of their especial mission, and was wondering how to escape from my awkward fix, when at that moment Miss Edith appeared."

"Laughing as usual, I suppose?" said Donald, a little bitterly, for he was beginning to think that his sister exhibited rather too much lightness of heart, in view of the gravity of her own situation, to say nothing of the dangers and hardships he was undergoing on her behalf.

"So far from it," replied the paymaster, "that there were traces of tears on her cheeks, and she was evidently suffering great mental distress.

"'Oh, Mr. Bullen!' she said in a low tone, so as not to be overheard by the savages, in case any of them understood English, 'I have just learned of something dreadful. This war-party is on its way to surprise Presque Isle, and capture the survivors of poor Mr. Cuyler's expedition, who have probably sought refuge there. Just think how terrible it would be if they should succeed, and our friends should be killed! Can't you do something to frustrate their wicked plan? You seem to have gained such an influence over them, I am sure you can if you only will.'

"I was rather staggered by this news, of course, and when she added: 'If you would only try, Mr. Bullen, and should succeed in saving the brave men in that fort, I should ever esteem you among the very dearest of my friends,' my resolution was instantly taken.

"I answered: 'For your sake, Miss Edith, I will make the effort and do what lies in my power to thwart the design of the red villains.' With that it was really touching to witness her gratitude and to hear her say that she should pray for my safety and success from that moment."

"She must have reasoned that I would be searching for her among Cuyler's fugitives and would very likely be in Presque Isle," reflected Donald.

"I don't see how that could be," retorted Bullen; "for I had carefully avoided any mention of your name, or of the fact that I had met you, thinking it useless cruelty to arouse her anxiety before your fate was definitely known."

"Which showed remarkable good sense on your part, and I thank you for your consideration," cried Donald. "Her anxiety then must have been for--"

"But how did you proceed to make good your promise?" interrupted Christie, hastily. "It seems to me you undertook a pretty big contract."

"So it was," responded the paymaster, "and in order to carry it out, I became, from that moment, an Indian of the Indians, a redskin of the redskins, and a savage of the savages. Why, for the sake of my paint I even gave up my daily tubbing, which, by the way, in my present position of deposed medicine man and white captive, I suppose I may have the melancholy satisfaction of resuming. I immediately agreed to accompany the war-party, telling them that, having once adopted the Indian costume, I had thereby cut myself off from all companionship with the whites. I promised to teach them the art of war as practised by the redcoats, and show them how to capture Presque Isle without the loss of a man."

"Oh you did, did you?" growled Christie.

"Yes, I did, and to begin with, I delayed their progress as much as possible, in the hope that Cuyler might reach you before we overtook him, and that you might join his retreat to Niagara. For this purpose I insisted that they carry along my tub, which, as I truly affirmed, contained all my medicine. Every morning when they were ready to start, I sat in it, under a closed tent of matting, and performed magic which they dared not interrupt. Sometimes the main body went on without us, so fearful were they of interfering with my mystic rites."

"What did you do under the tent?" asked Donald.

"Oh, just jabbered gibberish and rattled things and made smokes," replied the ex-medicine man.

"Then, when we reached Presque Isle and found it still occupied, I dissuaded them from an assault and proposed the scheme of a mine by which the fort might be destroyed without the loss of a warrior. According to their belief this mine was to run directly to the blockhouse, but I so laid it out that it should strike a building some distance away. Then I meant to collect all their powder, harmlessly explode it beneath the empty building, and thus leave them without means for prosecuting the fight. This plan miscarried through a cave-in of the roof, which showed them the true location of the mine's end and gave them a chance to set fire to the building nearest the blockhouse, which they hoped thus to destroy.

"When that plan failed, they continued the mine in the direction indicated by their new bearings and you would have been blown sky-high the moment it was completed, had I not persuaded them to first demand a surrender, and then wait until morning for your answer. Then I hoped, after getting you safely out of the place, with your arms and ammunition, under the pretence of surrendering, to harmlessly explode the mine, thus destroying all the enemy's powder, and leaving you masters of the situation. How that plan was frustrated, you know as well as I, though how the powder ever got moved and prematurely exploded, I never expect to discover unless you had a hand in it, Christie."

"No," replied the ensign, who had just received an expressive glance from Donald. "Neither I nor those with me had any definite knowledge of your mine before the explosion occurred."

"Well, however it was caused, my plans were completely defeated," said Bullen, "and not only that, but my reputation as a medicine man was ruined. As soon as we got to this place, a council was called, and I was charged with exploding the mine so as to destroy the Indians instead of the blockhouse. When I protested my innocence, they argued that I must, then, have lost my power over the fire-demon, and ordered me to repeat the magic tricks by which I had gained their confidence. You witnessed my humiliating failure, and its results; even my effervescing powders had become damp and failed to act.

"That is my story, gentlemen, and, if after hearing it, you still doubt my loyalty to the service to which we are all pledged, I can have no hope that others will believe me. In that case I have no desire to live and should make no struggle against the fate these savages contemplate for me. If, however, you can believe my story, wildly improbable as I know it must sound, then am I once more restored to life and hope."

As he thus concluded, the poor little man, grotesquely painted, battered, and bruised, turned a face of such intense pleading toward the comrades who had become his judges, that they both were moved by an overwhelming impulse to spring forward at the same moment and grasp his hands.

"We do believe you!" they cried.

"I am convinced," added Christie, "that you have acted as becomes an officer and a gentleman, Bullen, bravely and according to your best judgment for the honor and advancement of our cause. This I not only say now, but am prepared to state and maintain hereafter, officially and publicly, and there is my hand on it."

"And I say," cried Donald, "that you are a trump, Bullen, a genuine trump. Not only do I offer you my sincere friendship from this time forth, but I hereby pledge all the powers of the Metai--whatever that may be--so far as I can control them, and of the totem, whose emblem I wear, to your service!"

The effect of these hearty assurances of faith in him, and of continued friendship, was such that the little man's overstrained nerves suddenly gave way. He tried to speak, failed to utter a sound, and sank down sobbing like a child.

CHAPTER XXIX
DONALD AND THE PAYMASTER ESCAPE

While Donald's fears for Edith's safety were somewhat allayed by the paymaster's story, he was still very anxious concerning her. He knew nothing of Pontiac's friendly feeling toward his family, and feared that the prisoners were only being held on the island until it should be convenient to remove them to some distant Indian village, where, beyond the hope of rescue, they would be compelled to endure a life of slavery. Now, therefore, his desire was to return to the vicinity of the island, where he hoped to find some opportunity of escaping from his captors, and of effecting his sister's rescue. In his plans he of course included Christie and Bullen, whom he counted on for aid, though, to his chagrin, he was not allowed to communicate with them after that first interview. During it the leaders of the war-party also held a council, which resulted in a decision to proceed at once on their journey. Thus Bullen had hardly concluded his story, when camp was broken and the westward voyage was resumed. At the same time the three white men were separated and assigned to different canoes.

In their haste the Indians travelled early and late, with all speed. Both Christie and Bullen were compelled to assist in paddling, as well as to labor at the most menial tasks when in camp, receiving as a recompense only kicks and blows. They had, indeed, become slaves, and were treated as such, while at all times their tormentors found delight in assuring them that they would most certainly be burned to death on reaching the villages near Detroit. Fortunately game was plentiful, and food was procured in abundance by the hunters, otherwise the two slaves would have suffered from hunger, as they were never allowed to eat until the wants of every other person in the party had been amply supplied.

Donald, on the other hand, while watchfully guarded, was treated with the utmost of savage courtesy. He was not asked, nor even allowed, to perform any labor, was always supplied with the choicest food the camp afforded, and was the first to whom the calumet was handed upon the conclusion of a meal. In only two ways was he reminded of his true position. At night, though he was not bound, as were his comrades, he was obliged to sleep between two warriors, who were watchfully awake with every movement he made. If he attempted to hold converse with the other captives, they were driven from his presence with blows. Once, when he tried to communicate with Bullen, a young warrior sprang forward, struck the paymaster with a stick, and angrily bade him begone. Boiling with rage, and turning on the aggressor with clenched fists, Donald was about to avenge this insult, when he who had acted as interpreter sprang between them.

"My brother must be very careful," he said to Donald; "for some of our young men are so reckless that they do not even respect the Metai. If you should strike one of them, they would surely kill you and the other white men as well."

So Donald was obliged to control himself as best he could, and bear the sufferings of his companions in silence, but his mind was ever filled with plans for escape. Whenever he succeeded in attracting Christie's attention, he sought by meaning glances at a certain canoe smaller than any of the others, and then off over the lake, to convey an idea of what was in his mind, and was led to believe from the other's expression that he understood. From Bullen, however, he could gain no satisfaction in this way, and concluded that the paymaster was not so quick-witted as his brother officer.

At length one noon the war-party reached a point near the ruins of Sandusky, where they found a number of Shawnees, who were about to ascend Cedar Creek to their villages on the Scioto. These had with them several casks of rum, one of which was, after a long talk, transferred to the canoe in which Donald travelled. Then, to his intense grief and dismay, his own party resumed their journey, with the exception that Christie was left behind in the hands of the strangers. The slave had been sold, though he did not realize the fact until he started to enter the canoe in which he had come, and was forcibly restrained while it was pushed off. Then as the meaning of the situation flashed across him, he wrenched loose from those who held him and raced along the beach until opposite the canoe that held Donald, to whom he shouted:--

"Good-bye, Hester! God bless you! Tell them at the fort that I--"

Here he was pounced upon by his new masters and dragged away with Donald's answering farewell ringing in his ears.

It was after sunset that evening when the war-party reached the camp site selected as suitable for the orgy in which they proposed to indulge. The canoe containing Donald and the cask of fire-water was among the last to make a landing. Already fires were lighted on the bank above, and the earlier arrivals were impatiently awaiting the liquor for which they had been willing to barter a highly prized captive. Thus the moment it landed the cask was seized and borne triumphantly into camp, followed by all who had been on the beach. For the first time since his capture, Donald was left to himself, forgotten or overlooked in the general excitement. He stood for a minute, irresolute. His opportunity for escape had come. It would be easy to push off the canoe, jump in, and paddle away. To be sure, his absence would be quickly discovered and a hot pursuit would ensue, but he was willing to risk that. Or should he slip into the underbrush, take a great circuit about the camp and make his way to Detroit overland through the trackless forest? It would be a difficult but not impossible thing to do. Still, it must not be thought of, for there was Edith still a captive, and any freedom that he might gain must be devoted to her rescue. So he must take his chances of escape by water.

Donald was moving toward the canoe, when his steps were arrested by another consideration. What would become of Bullen? In their rage at the flight of one captive, the liquor-crazed savages would surely kill the other. Could he abandon a comrade to such a fate? Certainly not. If he escaped at all, it must be in company with the little paymaster who had proved himself so loyal. So this opportunity must be allowed to slip by, for poor Bullen was somewhere up there in the camp, cutting wood or performing other of the menial tasks allotted to him.

"No; old Bullen must not be deserted. There were but two of them left now, and they must stand by each other." Thus thinking, Donald turned toward the camp, but halted at the sound of approaching voices. Then two figures appeared through the dusk, both running, and one apparently pursued by the other. But one was swearing, and the other laughing. It was poor Bullen, clad in the ragged blanket,--which was now his sole garment,--sent down to fetch his own tub, to which one of the chiefs had taken such a fancy that he always sat in it before the evening camp-fires. The labor of carrying it up from the canoes at night, and back again in the morning devolved upon its original owner, who had thus come to hate it with a bitter hatred. This time he had purposely shirked the task of lugging the clumsy thing up that steep bank, and so had been sent back for it. The young guard who accompanied him was already exhilarated by a cup of fire-water, and in such haste to return for more that he found great delight in compelling his charge to run by prodding him from behind with a fish-spear.

As Donald was somewhat hidden in the shadow of a tree, neither of the newcomers noticed him, until the little paymaster had succeeded in getting the tub on his back, and started to retrace his weary way to the camp. Then, as Donald stepped from the shadow, Bullen, recognizing him, and instantly realizing their opportunity, turned like a flash, lunged forward with lowered head, and butted the young savage squarely in the stomach. He fell like a log, with his assailant and the tub on top of him. Ere he could regain his voice or breath, he was gagged, bound, and lifted into a canoe, which was immediately shoved off.

No word was spoken by either of the fugitives as the light craft shot away under the noiseless but powerful dips of their straining paddles; but, in spite of his anxiety, Donald could not help noticing and wondering at his comrade's proficiency in the art of canoeing. The painful lessons of his captivity had taught him how to escape from it; and he who two months before had never seen a birch canoe was now paddling one with the skill of an expert.

They were not gone from the beach more than five minutes, though their point of departure was already lost to view in the darkness, when a confusion of voices announced that their escape was discovered, and infused a new energy into their efforts. Donald was laying a course due west, and not more than a quarter of a mile from the beach. All at once he laid in his paddle, and said: "Face about carefully, Bullen, and help me chuck this useless weight overboard."

"Are you going to drown him?" asked the other, as he obeyed the order to face about.

"Not if I can help it; but we must take care that he doesn't drown us. He would be only too glad of a chance to upset the canoe; and he wouldn't have very hard work, either."

The getting of that young savage into the water was a difficult and ticklish job; but they finally succeeded, after Donald had first removed the gag from his mouth. He took the Indian's knife, and, as the latter slid into the water, Bullen held him by the scalp-lock, while Donald severed the thong that bound his wrists. In his rage, the Indian attempted to seize the gunwale of the canoe and pull it under; but, anticipating this, Donald struck him a rap on the head with the back of the knife that caused him to change his mind.

"Do you think he can swim with his feet bound?" asked Bullen, as the two white men resumed their paddling.

"Certainly he can," replied Donald; "and he can yell, too. Hear him?"

"I should say I did, and I wondered why you relieved him from that gag. If he keeps up that racket, he'll bring the whole fleet in this direction."

"That is exactly what I brought him along for, and what I want him to do," replied Donald, with a laugh. "Nor do I care how much longer they keep on in this direction, for I am about to take another. Don't you remember that we passed the island--a blue dot far out in the lake--this afternoon, so that it is now behind us and somewhere off in the northeast? We have got to run for it by the stars, and decide on our course before we entirely lose sight of the coast. Hush now, and don't speak another word for the next hour, as you value your life."

With this Donald steered the canoe, in a great sweeping curve, out into the vague blackness of the fresh-water sea.

CHAPTER XXX
IMMINENT DANGER OF THE SCHOONER GLADWYN

As the canoe containing Donald and the paymaster swept silently along through the darkness, its occupants heard the cries of the young Indian whom they had left in the water merge into a sound of other voices, showing that he had been discovered by his friends, and then all was quiet save for an occasional yell from the camp, where the fire-water was exerting its baneful influence. At length these, too, died into silence, the last glimmer of firelight was lost in the distance, and the fugitives felt that they might safely exult over their escape, though they still observed the precaution of speaking in the lowest of tones.

"Take a rest, Bullen," said Donald, breaking the enforced silence. "You must be pretty well exhausted with this work coming on top of what you've done all day, and it is no longer necessary for us to travel at full speed."

"I am about used up, that's a fact," admitted the little man, laying in his paddle and stretching himself wearily in the bottom of the canoe.

"I don't wonder. But I say I how like a trump you bowled that fellow over, on the beach. I was just wondering how we could down him without giving him a chance to alarm the camp, when all at once you had the job done. How did you happen to think of it?"

"I hadn't been thinking of anything else from the first," replied the paymaster, "and I knew your thoughts were running in the same direction, for I noticed the glances exchanged between you and Christie. Poor fellow! I wonder what will become of him."

"Yes. The dear old chap is in the worst of it now," sighed Donald. "We can only hope he'll be held for ransom or exchange. How I wish he were with us, not only for his own sake, but for the aid he could afford in the task we have undertaken."

"What task?"

"The rescue of my sister and Madam Rothsay, of course."

"You don't mean that you propose, unarmed and unaided, to attempt anything so hopeless as that?"

"Certainly I do. And that is what we are going to the island for. You wouldn't leave them in captivity, would you?"

"No, I wouldn't do that; but I would wait in hiding somewhere for the arrival of the reinforcements that must surely be coming up the lake by this time."

"And so give the Indians ample opportunity for removing their captives to some remote and inaccessible place, which I only hope they have not done already. No, indeed, that would never do. We must act promptly, and before those chaps on the island have a suspicion of our coming."

"But there are at least a dozen of them, and all are well armed."

"If there were twice as many I should still make the attempt to rescue my sister from their hands. Just imagine the distress she must be suffering all this time, uncertain as to her ultimate fate, dreading the worst, and hoping against hope, that some one will come to her assistance. Poor child! the suspense must be terrible."

"Yes," sighed Bullen. "And poor Madam Rothsay, too, plunged from the height of civilization into the depths of savagery without even a maid or a mirror. I can fully sympathize with her. But what do you propose to do? Have you thought out any plan?"

"I have thought of a great many; but only one of them appears at all feasible. It is that we advance boldly into the camp and demand that the ladies be at once taken to Detroit, or Fort Niagara if the Indians prefer, where we will promise that a goodly ransom shall be paid for them."

"As we have no means for enforcing such a demand, they will only laugh at us and add us to their list of captives."

"But we have the means of at least frightening them into compliance with our wishes. Are not you a great medicine man in their estimation, and capable of commanding the fire-demon? Am I not of the Totem of the Bear and wearer of the mystic emblem of the Metai? To be sure, I am very ignorant of these things, but we have had ample proof of their importance, and in the present case I propose to make the most of them."

"But, Hester, I can't appear before the ladies in this hideous costume. Do you realize that I am barefooted and literally bareheaded, while my only garment is a wretched old blanket, dirty and ragged, held in place by a rope of bark? I declare I don't think I have ever been so sorry for any one as I am for myself, when I reflect what an object for mirth I must appear. You should remember, too, that I have already gone through with a similar experience, which I have no desire to repeat."

"And came out of it with flying colors and waving plumes. Why, my dear fellow, those chaps on the island will delight in decorating, and befeathering, and fixing you up again in great shape, as they did before. You need not present yourself to the ladies until all your former gorgeousness is restored. Then imagine your triumph. You have no idea how becoming the costume of a forest warrior is to you. Don't you remember how highly Madam Rothsay complimented your impersonation of that character? But seriously, Bullen, I doubt if there is any other plan so good as the one I have suggested; and unless you can think of a better, it is the one we must adopt. Now, as we must be at least within sight of the island, and have no desire to pass it, or land on it in the dark, I propose that we get a little sleep while waiting for daylight to show us its position. My! won't I be glad of a breakfast, though? Plenty to eat was at least one alleviating feature of our recent captivity, and it is to be hoped that our new hosts will be equally generous with their provisions."

A few hours later Donald awoke with an uneasy motion of the canoe, to find it dancing on the little seas raised by a brisk breeze from the westward. The eastern sky was aglow; and, rising darkly against the ruddy light, not a mile away lay an island.

"Is that the one?" he asked of his companion, after awakening him, and pointing to the forest-crowned land.

"How should I know?" answered Bullen, sleepily. "They all look alike from this distance."

"All right," replied Donald, cheerily. "I'll put you so close to it that you can't help knowing." So saying, he seized his paddle and headed their craft toward the shore. He was weary and faint from hunger; but filled with an exhilaration born of near-by danger, and the possible meeting within a few minutes with the dearly loved sister whom he had sought so long, and for whose sake he had suffered so much.

They skirted the shore for a short distance before finding a little cove, bordered with overhanging spruce and cedars, at the head of which they made a landing on a beach of smooth pebbles.

"I believe this is the place," whispered the paymaster, visibly agitated by excitement.

The silence about them was unbroken, and if there were people near at hand, friends or foes, they gave no sign of their presence.

"Hello! Hello the camp!" called Donald, loud and clear. He had no idea of running the risk of being made a target for rifle bullets, by attempting to surprise an

Indian camp in broad daylight.

There was no response, no sound of any kind; and after waiting a full minute he sprang into a little path that wound upward among the evergreens, leaving Bullen to follow more slowly.

When the latter overtook his companion, a few moments later, he found him standing in an open space that he instantly recognized as the place where he had bidden farewell to Edith Hester some two weeks before. Now it was silent and deserted. The empty frames of a few lodges stood like gaunt skeletons of human habitations, and Donald was gazing wofully at the sodden ashes of a campfire.

"They are gone," he said, bitterly, "as I might have known they would be; and from the look of things they must have left very soon after you did. Now, if you can tell me which way to turn, or what to do next, you will prove yourself a better reader of riddles than I am."

"Find something to eat first, and plan afterwards," answered the little man, promptly. He could not help feeling relieved at escaping the ordeal of laughter he so much dreaded; and, though honestly sympathizing with Donald's keen disappointment, could think of nothing better to suggest at that moment than breakfast.

"I suppose you are right," agreed Donald, wearily, "and if you will start a fire I will see what I can provide in the way of food."

No hunter in those days travelled without a fire-bag containing flints, steel, and tinder; and, through all vicissitudes, Donald had retained the one that he had appropriated, together with his Indian costume, in the Wyandot camp. With this, then, Bullen started a fire, and finding a broken iron pot in the debris of the camp, cleaned it and set some water to boil.

In the meantime Donald, armed with the fish-spear that he had taken from the young Indian the night before, succeeded, within an hour, in killing a large fish, and a raccoon that he discovered digging for mussels on the beach.

When he returned with his trophies, Bullen greeted him with a joyous shout. "See what I have found!" he cried, at the same time holding up a small object that proved to be a cake of scented soap. It was one of a number that he had presented to the ladies when there before, and now it seemed to him even more precious than the welcome food procured by his companion.

After a hearty meal, that seemed to them one of the best they had ever tasted, in spite of the crudeness of its preparation, the little man treated himself to a bath in the lake, which he declared to be almost as good as a tub, after all. Before he emerged from it, he had succeeded, with the aid of his new-found treasure, in removing the last traces of savage paint from his body.

Then they discussed their situation and decided to make an effort to reach Detroit travelling only by night, and concealing themselves during the hours of daylight. They slept for the greater part of that day; and when, shortly before sunset, Donald visited the highest point of the island to scan the horizon in search of possible enemies, he had the bitter disappointment of seeing a distant sail, that must have passed close by the island, heading for the mouth of the Detroit river. It was the schooner that Gladwyn had sent to hasten Cuyler's movements, returning from the Niagara with the remnant of that expedition, and other reinforcements for the beleaguered post.

"If we had only kept watch!" he remarked to his companion, when telling him of what he had seen.

"Yes, if we only had!"

If they had, and had succeeded in gaining the vessel, it would probably never have reached Detroit; they, and every soul on board, would probably have been killed, and the whole course of events in that section of country would have been changed. Even as it was, the schooner was in most imminent danger; for her coming had been anticipated by Pontiac as well as by the garrison at Detroit, and every preparation known to that warlike chief had been made for her capture.

As she entered the river her every movement was watched by hundreds of gleaming eyes from the wooded banks, and when, with the dying out of the breeze, she was forced to drop anchor, it was with difficulty that the impatient warriors were persuaded from making an attack then and there.

CHAPTER XXXI
PONTIAC RECOGNIZES THE TOTEM

The vexatious calm lasted for two days. During this time the schooner caught only such puffs of wind as carried her a few miles up the river, and left her again

At War with Pontiac

anchored in the very narrowest part of the channel, still some ten miles below the fort. No sign of human presence had been discovered by those on board, no sound came from the solemn forests. Shy water-fowl swam fearlessly on the unruffled current that gurgled against the schooner's bow, and for aught their senses could discover, her people might have been the sole occupants of that beautiful, treacherous wilderness.

At sunset the distant boom of a heavy gun cheered their hearts with the knowledge that Detroit still held out, and redoubled their desire to gain its safe haven after their tedious voyage. Officers and men walked the deck impatiently, and searched the sky for wind clouds, while the sailors whistled shrilly for a breeze. But none came and the night descended calm, dark, and still. As the slow hours dragged themselves away, the ship's company, weary of the monotony of their watch, sought their sleeping places, or found such scant comfort as the decks afforded, until of them all only the sentry was awake.

Still the schooner was not unprepared for an attack. Her broadside guns were loaded to the muzzle with grape and musket balls. Every man on board was armed, even as he slept, and her only danger lay in being boarded by an overwhelming number of the enemy, against whom the heavy guns would thus be rendered ineffective. But the night wore on, and he made no sign. The sentry relieved at midnight reported no cause for alarm. The one who went off duty two hours later gave a similar assurance of continued safety. His successor yawned sleepily as he paced to and fro, and shivered with the chill that had crept into the night. A slight mist was rising from the water, and through it even the black outline of the forest was undistinguishable. As nothing could be seen, the sentry gave over his pacing, and, leaning against the foremast, devoted himself to listening. He even closed his eyes to improve his hearing, and so stood halt musing, half dreaming of his distant English home, until, suddenly from out of the blackness, there rang a shout of warning. It was instantly followed by another, and a confused tumult on the water at no great distance.

As the startled sentry echoed the alarm and sprang to the bulwarks, he caught a glimpse of moving objects sweeping down on the slumbering vessel. In another minute the enemy would have swarmed irresistibly over her sides, and her fate would have been sealed. But, ere half that time had elapsed, there burst from her such a blaze of cannon and musketry that the night was illumined as though by a flash of lightning. The schooner trembled to her keel with the concussion. The advancing canoes were so torn and riddled, by the hail of grape and bullets, that several of them sank, a score of their occupants were killed, many more were wounded, and the survivors fled in consternation to the shore. From there, behind a breastwork of logs, they opened a harmless fire that was quickly silenced by the schooner's guns. Soon afterwards, a favoring breeze springing up, she weighed anchor and made her way in safety to the fort, to which she brought not only reinforcements of troops, but a supply of ammunition and provisions, without which the garrison must speedily have surrendered.

On the very night of all these happenings, the canoe containing Donald Hester and Paymaster Bullen entered the Detroit river, and began to stem its swift current, moving silently and in blackest shadows. Hoping to run the long gantlet of the channels, and reach the fort before daylight, they strained every nerve to the attainment of this purpose. They, too, had heard the defiant boom of the distant sunset gun, announcing to all the forest world that Detroit was still held for England's king, and the sound gave them a new courage.

They had paddled for hours, and knew that midnight must be long past, when, without the warning of sight or sound, they suddenly discovered their craft to be surrounded by moving shadows. These were canoes headed across the stream, and instantly Donald turned his craft in the same direction, as though it belonged to the ghostly fleet. It was a terrible situation, and one in which the slightest mistake would prove fatal. Donald noticed Bullen's start on the discovery of their danger, and blessed him for the coolness with which he continued the noiseless dip of his paddle. His hope was to work toward the outer edge of the fleet, and then slip away in the mist-clouds that were rising thinly from the water before the other side of the river should be reached. At the same time he wondered where these canoes could have come from, and what was the cause of their mysterious movements; for, thinking that the schooner he had seen two days before must long since have reached the fort, it did not occur to him that she could be the object of attraction.

Bullen was the first to see it. With a choking gasp he leaned back and whispered hoarsely, "The schooner! We must warn them!"

"Certainly," replied Donald, promptly, as though it were a matter of course that they should sacrifice themselves to save their friends. Then he raised a shout so loud and far-reaching that it seemed as though it must be heard even at the distant fort. It was instantly echoed by another from Bullen. Then an Indian canoe crashed into theirs, and in a moment they were struggling with half a dozen infuriated savages. Ere the struggle was concluded, there came a blaze of fire, a crash of thunder, the rending of wood, shrieks, and yells. To Donald also came oblivion; while Bullen first found himself in the water, then dragged from it into a canoe, and a moment later a helplessly bound captive at the mercy of an enraged foe.

The failure of his carefully planned attack on the schooner was a bitter blow to Pontiac, the haughty chieftain, who was striving to drive the red-coated invaders from the land still claimed by his people. The prize for which he had schemed and fought so long had been within his grasp only to be snatched away at the last moment. Already had his war-parties captured all the British posts west of the Niagara save only Detroit and Fort Pitt. Already was the crimson wave of war lapping the frontier settlements, and driving them back. Thus far his warriors had been everywhere victorious, and this was their first repulse. Could he have captured that schooner with all that it contained, and turned its guns against the slight defences of Detroit, that place must speedily have fallen. Then, with his entire force, he would have been free to sweep resistlessly down the Alleghany to lower the last English flag west of the mountains. But his certain victory had been turned into disaster by a cry of warning from the very midst of the attacking fleet. It was incredible! Who had uttered that cry? What had come over his warriors, that such a thing could be possible? In his rage, Pontiac ordered that the prisoners be securely guarded until he could invent some punishment adequate to their offence. Should they escape, it should be meted out to their guards. Then, too, let the warriors who had admitted those white men to their ranks look to themselves; for if any were found who had played traitor, their fate should be such that for generations the mere telling of it would chill the blood of all hearers. Thus spake Pontiac, and the forest warriors trembled before the wrath of their mighty chief.

On the following day he sat moodily in his lodge on a small island at the head of the river, whither he was accustomed to retreat for quiet and meditation. Only his favorite daughter was with him, and she was striving in vain to find words of comfort that should banish the dark cloud from his face. To this place, according to his order, were brought the prisoners who had defeated his plan of attack on the schooner, that he might pronounce judgment upon them. One lay on the ground before the entrance to the lodge, covered with blood and apparently lifeless, while the other, clad in a tattered blanket and tightly bound, stood dejectedly beside him.

"Why bring ye dead men to this place?" demanded Pontiac, spurning the prostrate form with his foot. "Take the scalp, and throw the body to the fishes."

"He is not dead. He still breathes," answered one of the warriors who had brought the prisoners.

"It matters not. Still do as I said."

As the warrior drew his scalping-knife and stooped to obey, the Indian girl, leaning forward to obtain a better view of him whose case was thus summarily disposed, uttered a cry of dismay, grasped the warrior's arm, and spoke a few hurried words to her father.

[Illustration: Pontiac discovers that Donald is tattooed with the Magic Circle.]

The great chief started, drew his own knife, and knelt beside the unconscious form. The other Indians imagined he was about to slay the youth with his own hand, and thus avenge the grievous injury inflicted upon their cause. Instead of so doing, Pontiac merely slit open the sleeve of Donald's hunting-shirt, and gazed intently for a moment at the mark thus disclosed. His stern face grew almost tender with the remembrance of the laughing child who had saved his own life so many years before. Then rising, and turning to his warriors, he said:--

"He is of the Totem of the Bear, and is sealed with the symbol of the magic circle. We may not kill him, for he is favored of the Great Spirit. Lift him within the lodge, and keep to yourselves the secret of his presence in this place.

"As for this other,"--here he gazed sternly at poor Bullen, who, while rejoicing that the mystical marking on his friend's arm seemed about to do him good service once more, wished he knew what was to be his own fate. "As for this other," repeated Pontiac, "this hairless dog of an Englishman, take him to the Ottawa village, and deliver him to the tormentors, nor ever let me set eyes on him again."

Thus saying, the chieftain, whose commands none dared disobey, entered the lodge whither Donald had been tenderly conveyed, and where the chief's daughter was already bathing his wounds.

Then the others seized the little paymaster, hurried him to the canoe in which he had been brought, and departed with all speed for the Ottawa village, which was located near the river bank some two miles above the fort. Here the arrival of the prisoner, and the announcement of the sentence passed upon him, was received with yells of approval and every manifestation of savage joy. But there were some who shook their heads dubiously. They were of the war-party recently returned from Presque Isle; and, recalling the marvellous things done by this white medicine man, they were still fearful of his power. The majority, however, paid slight attention to these croakers, and the work of preparation for the forthcoming spectacle was pushed with eager haste.

CHAPTER XXXII
LAST CRUISE OF THE PAYMASTER'S TUB

While the preparations for Paymaster Bullen's martyrdom were in progress, his bonds were removed, and he was supplied with food that he might gain strength the longer to endure the proposed torture. He was allowed to sit in the shade of a tree, where he was guarded by two stalwart warriors, not so much to prevent his escape, as to restrain the inquisitive spectators who thronged about him. These were roused to such a pitch of fury at the sight of one who had frustrated their long-cherished plan for capturing the schooner, that, had they been allowed, they would have torn him in pieces. Many of these were women, who mocked at and reviled the unfortunate Englishman, screaming like so many furies, spitting at him, and gloating over his miserable plight, as is the custom of a certain grade of womankind all over the world. Inspired by the example of their elders, a swarm of impish children added their shrill cries to the tumult, let fly an occasional blunt-headed arrow at the helpless captive, or darted between the legs of the guards in their efforts to strike him. Finally the exasperated warriors turned on this petty rabble and with stern words bade them begone.

Others came for a look at the prisoner while he ate, and among them he recognized the Zebra. This man he addressed in English, asking him what was to be his fate, but the Indian only laughed and turned away. Then came the young warrior whom he and Donald had thrown overboard a few nights before, other members of the party with which he had travelled to Presque Isle, and still others whom he recognized, until it seemed as though every Indian he had ever seen had come to witness his execution.

He knew it was to be an execution, and that he had naught in prospect save death; but he hoped this might come speedily, and that in whatever shape it approached, he might be given strength to meet it as became one of his race and position. He had heard his branch of the service spoken of lightly because physical courage was not supposed to be among its requirements. Now he was to be given the opportunity for proving that a staff officer could die as bravely as one of the line. If only they would not burn him to death, as had been threatened. It seemed as though he could bear anything else, but that was too horrible.

His melancholy reflections were interrupted by the passing of a noisy group surrounding two who bore some burden. As they neared him, Bullen saw with amazement that it was the bath-tub of which he had been so proud, which had been the source of so much pleasure, in which he had suffered, and the loss of which had been a source of genuine grief. It had evidently been retained by the Indians as a novel trophy, and was as evidently to be connected in some manner with his approaching fate. The tub was carried beyond his sight, and a few minutes later he was led to the end of a long, narrow lane, bordered by two living walls of human beings. Then he knew that he was to undergo the terrible ordeal of the gantlet, which had been so often described to him that he felt familiar with all its sickening details.

The entire population of the village was ranged in two parallel rows facing each other, and all were armed with sticks, clubs, dog-whips or some similar weapon with which to strike at the poor wretch who would be forced to run for his life down the dreary lane.

As Bullen faced this ordeal he recalled how other men had acted under similar circumstances. Some had been beaten to death ere completing half the course; while others had been so fleet of foot as to escape almost unhurt. One, he remembered, was a tall man of such strength and agility that he snatched a club from the nearest Indian at the moment of starting and brandished it with such effect as he ran that no one dared strike him.

But the paymaster was neither tall, nor strong, nor agile. He was short and stout. As for running, he had not done such a thing since he was a child, nor even then that he could remember. Now it would certainly kill him to run for even a short distance, while he would as certainly be killed if he did not run. The little man was in despair; it was so pitiful and mean a fate to be beaten to death with clubs like a mad dog--oh! if he only were one, how he would scatter that throng of howling savages. With this thought an inspiration came to him like a ray of sunlight piercing the blackness of a dungeon. He felt among the inner folds of his ragged blanket, withdrew a small object and thrust it into his mouth. A second later the blanket was snatched from his body leaving him clad only in a breech clout, and he was given a push into the lane as a hint that his time for running had come.

A hush of expectancy fell upon the eager throng, and each grasped his stick more firmly with the resolve to have at least one good cut at that bald-headed white man as he ran or staggered past. The first one on the right, who happened to be the Zebra, lifted a switch and struck the paymaster a smart though not a cruel blow across the shoulders as an intimation that the fun had begun.

The first one on the left, a burly black-browed giant who hated all white men with a bitter hatred, raised a heavy club with a vicious swing. Ere it could descend Bullen sprang at him and blew from his mouth a cloud of froth full in the giant's face. The latter staggered back, dropped his club, clapped both hands to his eyes and uttered a yell of terror. Then the little man folded his arms and walked composedly down the long lane, making a snarling, gurgling noise in his throat and frothing at the mouth as though he had indeed been smitten with the peculiar form of madness for which he had just wished.

A great fear fell on the assemblage as one and all recalled the tales of this white man's magic power. Not a hand was lifted against him as he passed, and the awe-stricken savages drew back at his approach as though he had been plague-stricken. So he made his unmolested way to the very end of the lane, his enemies parting before him, but crowding behind and following him with an eager curiosity.

At length he paused and gazed with mingled horror and rage at something that barred his further progress. On two logs, between which burned a small fire, was set his own bath-tub. The water with which it was half filled was just beginning to simmer, and near at hand was a pile of dry wood cut into short lengths. In an instant the awful meaning of these preparations flashed across his mind. They intended to boil him alive! For a moment he felt sick and dizzy. All things spun in a mad whirl before his blurred vision, and he feared his senses were departing. Recovering himself by a supreme effort of will, and animated by an access of fury, he sprang forward, overturned the tub, so that its contents were poured on the hissing flames, instantly extinguishing them, and hurled it to one side. Then clearing his mouth of the last of the frothy matter which had been produced by chewing a bit of soap, the little man turned and confronted his tormentors.

Angry murmurs rose among them and deepened into a confused clamor. Some were for killing him at once, but the majority dared not. Neither were they willing that he should go free, nor was one found bold enough to adopt him as husband, brother, or son, as by Indian custom any had the right to do who felt so inclined. The discussion was finally ended by the black-browed giant who had been the object of Bullen's attack and who still smarted from the indignity. Silencing the clamor, with an authoritative voice, he proposed a plan that was unanimously adopted.

A minute later another white man, whom to his amazement the paymaster recognized as his long lost "Tummas," was dragged and pushed through the throng. In his hands he bore several pots of paint and a number of rude brushes. Now he was ordered to begin work at once on his former master and decorate him in the highest style of savage art.

"Oh Lawk, Muster Bullen! To think we should never ha come to this," gasped the trembling man as he prepared to obey this mandate. "Hi opes has you won't lay it hup against me, sir, if Hi do as Hi'm bid: for if Hi don't jump spry the creeters will kill me, 'deed they will, sir."

"Tummas," answered the little man, severely, "since you seem to have accepted service with these heathen savages, it becomes you to do their bidding without hesitation; but I never expected to see a respectable English valet sink so low, I certainly never did."

"Oh Lawk, Muster Bullen! Hi opes, sir, as you don't think Hi've done such a think of my hown free will. No, sir. Hindeed Hi 'aven't: but Hi'm compelled, sir. Hi 'as to paint 'em and likewise shave their 'eads and look after their nasty 'air. Yes, sir, and many a think besides that you wouldn't believe. But some day Hi'll pizen 'em, sir, or spiflicate 'em in their sleep, the hopportunity for which is the honly pleasure in life Hi 'as to look forward to, sir."

As "Tummas" uttered these fierce words he drew several vicious streaks of red across the paymaster's body, for he was already hard at work at his unwelcome task.

So by the liberal application of pigments and feathers, poor Bullen was once more got up in savage guise. Then he was bound hand and foot so that he could not move, gagged so that he could utter no sound, placed in his once beloved, but now hated tub, borne to the water's edge, and set afloat on the swift current, followed by derisive yells from his enemies.

That same afternoon Major Gladwyn, who was standing on one of the water bastions of Fort Detroit, in company with a lady, descried a suspicious object floating down the river and called for a spy-glass. Gazing intently through it, he exclaimed: "Pon my soul, madam, I believe we are here just in time to interrupt another attempt of those villanous redskins to destroy my schooners. They have already tried fire-rafts and other infernal devices without number, but always at night. Now, if I'm not mistaken, they have the audacity to try again in broad daylight, thinking no doubt to catch us napping. But I'll teach them that we are wide awake at all hours. That is certainly an Indian in full paint and feathers, though what he is floating on I can't make out. Orderly, bring me my long range rifle--will you take this glass, madam, and watch the effect of my shot? It may prove interesting as well as pleasing after your recent terrible experience."

By the time Madam Rothsay succeeded in focusing the glass on the approaching object, Major Gladwyn was carefully sighting his rifle.

Suddenly she uttered a cry of dismay. "For Heaven's sake, don't fire, major! It is poor, dear Paymaster Bullen. At least that is his tub; and he was arrayed in that very same remarkable costume the last time I saw him."

"Impossible, madam! An officer in His Majesty's service!"

"Indeed, it is possible, major; and I beg you to send out a boat. Fill it with armed men, if you like; but I beg and implore you not to act hastily."

Only half convinced that he was acting prudently, Major Gladwyn yielded to Madam Rothsay's pleadings, and did as she suggested. To make sure that no mistakes were committed, he accompanied the boat, with his rifle, loaded and cocked, held ready for instant use.

A few minutes later, the tub with its helpless occupant was cautiously towed to the shore; but not until the gag was removed from his mouth, and they heard the little paymaster's fervent "Thank God!" could either the major or his soldiers believe that their prize was a white man.

As he landed and his bonds were loosed, the newcomer turned and thrust his hated tub out into the stream with such savage energy that the water poured over its side, it filled, and, with a gurgling rush of air-bubbles, sank beneath the swift current.

Then the little man's overtaxed strength gave way. He took a few uncertain steps, tried to apologize, reeled, and fell limply into the arms of the nearest bystander, who happened to be Madam Rothsay herself.

CHAPTER XXXIII
FORT DETROIT IS REINFORCED

From the very first the two tribes of Wyandots and Pottawattamies had been but lukewarm allies of the Ottawas in the prosecution of this war. Their chiefs were jealous of Pontiac and yielded obedience to his orders rather through fear than from any real loyalty to his cause. Still, so long as his plans were successful, his arms victorious, and his appeared to be the winning side, they were content to follow his leadership. No sooner, however, did the tide of fortune turn against him with the failure of his attempt to capture the schooner, than these tribes sent a deputation of chiefs to Gladwyn with proposals for peace. This was granted them and the treaty was consummated by a general exchange of prisoners.

It was owing to Pontiac's distrust of these allies, to whom had been intrusted the attack on Cuyler's expedition, that he had secretly sent Ah-mo and Atoka to provide for the safety of Edith Hester, rightly thinking that they could act more effectively than a larger party and at the same time attract less notice. How they succeeded in conveying their charge to an island on which was maintained a picket of Ottawa warriors, has already been told.

This picket post was a source of grievance to the Wyandots, who, dwelling nearest the mouth of the river, claimed that they alone were entitled to occupy that territory and guard its approaches. After their victory over Cuyler, they protested so loudly against the continuation of the Ottawa outpost on their island, that Pontiac reluctantly ordered it to be withdrawn, and the captives who were held there to be brought to his own village.

Thus it happened that to these Indians was left the entire guarding of the southern approaches to Detroit; and when, at the end of July, a strong detachment of troops in twenty-two bateaux, under command of Captain Dalzell, appeared at the mouth of the river, they having just concluded their treaty of peace, allowed it to pass up unmolested. The flotilla came up at night; and at sunrise, as the sea of fog covering the vicinity of Detroit began to roll away in fleecy masses, its foremost boats were discovered by a sentinel, who at once announced the joyful intelligence. As before, the beleaguered garrison hastened to the water front in anxious expectancy. Were the approaching boats indeed filled with friends come to their relief, or, as in the former case, with victorious savages and dejected captives? Not until the questioning salute of their guns was answered by the glad roar of a swivel from the foremost boat was the query answered, and the apprehensions of the war-worn garrison changed to a joyous certainty.

All at once their rejoicings were silenced by a double sheet of fire that leaped from both banks of the river at once. A hail of bullets was poured into the crowded boats from among the buildings and orchards of the French farmers, and many a red-coated soldier fell beneath the fire of a foe whom he could neither see nor reach.

Pontiac had been warned at last of this new danger, and had sent his trusty Ottawas, leaping like deer, down the river banks with a faint hope that the approaching convoy might still be cut off. But they were too late, and though their fire was very destructive while it lasted, the boats pressed steadily on and in a few minutes more had gained the shelter of the fort.

The newly arrived detachment--three hundred strong--was composed of troops from the 50th and 80th regiments of the line, and twenty of Rogers' hardy rangers. As boat after boat swept up to the strand and landed its men they were received with wild cheers, frantic embraces, and every manifestation of overwhelming joy. The new-comers, sturdy, well-fed, and perfectly equipped, presented a striking contrast to the gaunt, hollow-cheeked troops clad in tatters, who had held the fort so long and so bravely. As the former moved steadily up the narrow street in a long line of glittering scarlet, while drum and fife waked cheery echoes from the silent houses, the latter felt that the day of their deliverance had indeed come, and well repaid for all their toil.

Dalzell's boats brought many things besides men, guns, and ammunition. It brought provisions, letters, and news from the great far-away world. It brought a confirmation of the treaty, recently signed between England and France, which set at rest all fears that Pontiac might receive French aid in his present struggle. It also brought a number of dainties for the officers' mess, such as had been unknown to its table for many months. So Gladwyn gave a dinner that night to which every officer in the fort was bidden.

When the appointed time arrived and Majors Gladwyn and Rogers; Captains Dalzell, Grant, and Gray; Lieutenants Cuyler, Hay, and Brown, and half a dozen more, all in speckless uniforms, were assembled about the homely but well-laden mess-table, there entered still another at whom the newcomers gazed in surprise but without recognition. He was a little man dressed in the costume of the backwoods, a belted buckskin shirt, leggings, and moccasins, and a coonskin cap. He hesitated, as though from shyness, as he glanced irresolutely about him. Then Gladwyn, stepping quickly forward, took him by the hand, exclaiming:--

"You are just in time, my dear fellow, though I had begun to fear that you were not going to join us. Here are a lot of old friends waiting to greet and congratulate you."

"Are they?" asked the stranger, dubiously.

"By Jove!" laughed Gladwyn, "I don't believe one of them recognizes you. Gentlemen, permit me the honor of introducing one of the heroes of this present war, Paymaster Leonidas Bullen."

Whereupon there arose such a shout from that mess-room as startled the distant sentries on the outer walls. "Bullen, old man, forgive me." "It can't be!" "Incredible!" "Bullen, the Beau Brummel of the service, in leather!" "Why, Diogenes, what are you doing here?" "Is it a masquerade?" "Is it a joke?" "What means this unique headgear?" "And Diogenes, I say, where is the tub?"

"Gentlemen," replied the paymaster, "it is no joke, but a stern reality. As my only choice of a dinner dress lay between a suit of paint and this costume, out of consideration for your prejudices I chose this. My head-gear may be unique, but it is at least warm and it is also the only covering I can at present bestow upon my baldness. It is true I might have worn feathers, but unfortunately feathers suggest to me only very recent and unpleasant associations. As for my tub, I shall consider it a personal favor, gentlemen, if you will never again mention that unfortunate article in my presence."

"He came very near being boiled alive in it," whispered Gladwyn to Captain Dalzell.

"What?"

"Yes, like a prawn or a crayfish."

"By Jove! How?"

Then Gladwyn related the history of the paymaster's recent experiences and bravery so effectively that the poor little man became rosy with confusion, and when at the conclusion of the narrative his health was pledged with a round of cheers, he could only stammer in reply:--

"I thank you, gentlemen, from the bottom of my heart. I also thank the major for his kindly effort to convert me into a hero. I fear, though, that he is only trying to make amends for threatening to shoot me when I first made application for his hospitality."

"Shoot you, old man! You don't mean it. What for? Had you challenged him? Tell us about it."

"It is only too true," confessed Major Gladwyn, "and but for the timely interference of Madam Rothsay I fear I should have succeeded to my everlasting sorrow."

When this had been explained, and Madam Rothsay's health had been pledged, Captain Dalzell inquired what had become of Miss Hester, who, he understood, had accompanied the elder lady on her western trip.

"I am sorry to say," replied Gladwyn, "that she is held prisoner by Pontiac in company with her father the major, and Ensign Hester her brother. He was with Bullen, you know, and sacrificed himself to warn the schooner of her danger the other night. It was a fine thing to do, and I would gladly give up the schooner, valuable as she is to me, if by so doing he could be restored to us. Madam Rothsay was also held prisoner by the redskins until it fortunately occurred to them to offer her in exchange for a villanous Ojibwa chief, whom we happened to have on hand. Of course I was only too glad to make the exchange, and wish I had a dozen more like him to offer for the Hesters."

"By Jove!" cried Captain Dalzell, "it is horrible to think of the grand old major and his lovely daughter, and that fine son of his, all in the power of those devils. Can't we do something toward their rescue, Gladwyn? Surely we are strong enough now to take the offensive. I should be only too happy to lead a night attack on Pontiac's camp. We could make it a complete surprise, and my fellows are simply spoiling for a fight. It does seem as though the time to strike a decisive blow had come, and every day that we postpone it only increases the peril of the Hesters. What do you say, major? Won't you consider the proposition seriously?"

So the dinner party was turned into a council of war, and, before it broke up, an attack on Pontiac's camp had been arranged for the following night.

CHAPTER XXXIV
AH-MO, THE DAUGHTER OF PONTIAC

The day just concluded had been one of unhappiness and anxiety for the great Ottawa chieftain. The rumored defection of his Wyandot allies was proved true. The safe arrival at the fort of Dalzell's expedition was the most deadly blow yet struck at his cherished project. To crown all, he was not on the best of terms with his sole remaining allies, the fierce and warlike Ojibwas. These had no more desire than the Wyandots to fight on a losing side; and, moreover, they had a private grievance of long standing against Pontiac. It arose from the capture of one of their chiefs by the English, and the refusal of Pontiac to offer Major Hester in exchange for him.

Firm in his belief that Detroit must eventually fall into his hands, and that every soul within its walls would be killed, the Ottawa chief, intent on saving the life of the white man who had once saved his, refused to restore him to a place of such peril. In vain did the Ojibwa captive--who was no other than our old acquaintance, Mahng--send messages by the French settlers, who carried occasional communications between the fort and the Ottawa village, threatening that, if Major Hester were not exchanged for him, he would influence his tribe to make peace with the

English. Pontiac only sent answer that the major was not his prisoner, but his guest, and therefore not subject to exchange, but that the first captive of sufficient consequence who should be brought in should be offered in his place.

When, therefore, Edith Hester and Madam Rothsay reached the village, Pontiac conceived the project of presenting the latter before the gates of Detroit, and demanding the release of the Ojibwa chief in her stead. To the grief of Madam Rothsay herself, and of the beautiful charge from whom she was thus separated, this plan was at once carried out, with the result that Mahng was restored to his followers. He was, however, more imbittered than ever against Pontiac, not only on account of his long imprisonment, but because of a woman having been offered and accepted in exchange for him.

This was not only a severe blow to his own pride, but to that of his people; and they became clamorous to have the insult avenged, for which purpose Mahng demanded that Major Hester be delivered to them, to do with as they pleased. This demand was refused with such indignant scorn that Mahng's evil face became black with fury; and, though he strode from Pontiac's presence in silence, his heart was filled with rage. This was intensified a few days later when the Ottawa chief upbraided him, and charged him with superstitious cowardice for aiding the escape of a white prisoner who had been condemned to death. In this case, Mahng had felt certain that Paymaster Bullen, carefully disguised as an Indian, would be fired upon and killed by the garrison of the fort, as he approached it, and was as disgusted as any one could be by the unexpected result of that experiment.

Distressed as Edith Hester was at being separated from Madam Rothsay, she rejoiced at the latter's restoration to the protection of British troops, and became reconciled to her own prolonged captivity when she found that she was to be allowed to spend it in the company of her beloved father.

Although the brave old major chafed like a caged lion at his enforced detention in Pontiac's camp, he bore it without a murmur, and strove to aid the cause of his countrymen by endeavoring to impress upon the Ottawa leader the folly of resistance to the English. He knew nothing of his daughter's captivity, nor even of her departure from New York, until one evening, as he sat alone in the room assigned to his use, the door was gently opened, and she stood before him in all the radiancy of her youth and beauty. For a moment he stared as though at a vision, but as she stepped forward he opened wide his arms, and father and daughter were reunited in a fond embrace. There were so many questions to be asked and answered, so much news to be told, and so many conjectures to be made concerning their ultimate fate, that, for more than an hour, they talked oblivious of everything, save the joy of being together. Then Edith exclaimed in dismay:--

"If I haven't forgotten poor Ah-mo, and left her waiting outside all this time, when I said I'd be back in a few minutes! May I fetch her, father? She is one of my dearest friends, and I want you to know her."

"Certainly, my dear," answered the major, with a smile. "Bring her in, by all means; for any friend of yours must needs be a friend of mine as well."

A moment later, when the Indian girl, who had waited patiently all this time, was led into the bare little room, it was Edith's turn to be surprised. Instead of receiving her as a stranger, Major Hester greeted her as a friend whose absence had been a source of genuine regret.

"It is good to see you once more, Ah-mo," he said. "Though, had I known the nature of the errand that caused your absence, my anxiety for your return had been doubled many times. Now I have to bless you and thank you for your brave care of my dear girl, who has, all unknown to me, passed through so many recent perils."

"Then you knew Ah-mo before, papa!" exclaimed Edith; "and all this time she never told me."

"Nor did she tell me that she was going in search of you, for which I am now grateful, since it saved me a painful anxiety," replied the major. "Yes; Ah-mo and I are old friends, and, of late, many an hour, that would otherwise have hung heavily on my hands, has been lightened by her visits. Forest maiden as she is, I find her to be well versed in polite literature, and possessed of a shrewd knowledge of affairs, though, above all, has she learned the value of a silent tongue."

"Yes, indeed!" cried impulsive Edith. "Even during our short acquaintance I have discovered that, in many things which I ought to know, her knowledge is superior to mine; that for keeping a secret she has no equal; and that with it all she is one of the dearest and sweetest and most lovable girls I ever met."

Then, seeing that her friend was covered with confusion by all this praise, she hastened to change the subject by saying, "And now, if Donald were only here, what a happy party we would form, and how readily might we forget our captivity!"

"Not captivity!" interrupted Ah-mo, eagerly. "Pontiac's guests can never be his captives."

"While your father's opinions and mine are not agreed on that point, my dear girl, he certainly has done everything suggested by a courteous hospitality to make my stay here comfortable," said Major Hester. "But, as any form of detention against one's will must be regarded as a captivity, I cannot echo your wish, Edith, that Donald were here. He is so young, so fearless, and so impatient of inaction, that, were he taken prisoner, he would do and dare anything to effect an escape, with possible results that I cannot bear to contemplate. Therefore I am glad that he is far away, and is happily free from a knowledge of our position."

"Why, father, is he not in Detroit?" queried Edith.

"No; he left before the outbreak, with despatches for New York, and, had you not come by the north shore of the lake, he would surely have met you."

"Well," sighed Edith, "I wish we might have met. Had I known of his coming, I should certainly have waited for him in New York; though, as things have turned out, I wouldn't have missed this coming to you, father dear, for the world. Now I only hope he won't try to return before peace is declared. Oh, Ah-mo! why will your father persist in this horrid war? He surely cannot hope to succeed against the forces of the king."

"His warriors have not yet been defeated," replied the Indian girl quickly, with a bright flush heightening the dark beauty of her face. "And he is too brave a man not to make war against those who would steal the lands of his people, and kill them like so many wild beasts. Why do the English drive my father to war?"

"Do not become involved in fruitless discussion, my dears," chided the old soldier. "This question is one to be settled by older and wiser heads than yours."

So the conversation was changed, and ran in other channels far into the night.

By Pontiac's order, suitable accommodations had been provided for Edith in the farmhouse adjoining that occupied by her father, and, at her request, Ah-mo shared them with her at night. During the day the latter was much with her own father, acting as his secretary and adviser, for which position no one of Indian blood was so well fitted as she.

Pontiac was too able a man not to realize the value of an education beyond that afforded by the forest, and had long ago selected Ah-mo, the cleverest of all his children, as the one who should receive its benefits. So she had spent six years in Montreal, studying diligently, learning easily, and in all ways preparing herself for the very place she now occupied. She had been courted, petted, and made much of by the gay society of the Canadian capital; but never did she forget her loyalty to her own people. Thus, when, on the eve of his great undertaking, her father sent for her, she unhesitatingly relinquished the allurements of civilization for a place in his wilderness lodge and by his side.

From him she was now learning the greatest of all arts, that of knowing when to keep silence and when to speak. Thus, fond as she had become of Edith Hester, she wisely kept many things from her; among others, by Pontiac's desire, the fact that her brother Donald and Paymaster Bullen had been captured, an event that occurred some two weeks after Edith herself was brought from the island. Nor were the major and his daughter allowed to know what took place in the Ottawa village, which had been removed a full mile from the carefully guarded quarters assigned to them, and to which, for their own safety, they were closely confined.

Ah-mo's influence over her father was regarded unfavorably by some of the chiefs, and especially by Mahng, the Ojibwa, who, having sought her in marriage for his son Suggema, and being met with a prompt refusal, had conceived an intense dislike for her. This was inflamed by her friendship for the daughter of Major Hester, whom Mahng regarded as the chief of his enemies. Therefore, in all his plans for revenge upon those who he was determined should feel the weight of his wrath, Ah-mo was included; and he impatiently awaited a fitting time for the carrying out of his evil designs. When, therefore, near the close of a certain day, Pontiac bade the Ojibwas hold themselves in readiness to repel an attack, which he had secret information the English were to make that night, Mahng smiled grimly; for he believed his long-desired opportunity had arrived.

CHAPTER XXXV
A NIGHT OF FIGHTING AND TERROR

In Fort Detroit the night after that of Gladwyn's dinner party was one of sleeplessness, busy preparation, and intense, though suppressed excitement. The expe-

At War with Pontiac

dition intended for the surprise and destruction of Pontiac's village, and the rescue of the Hesters, was about to set forth under command of Captain Dalzell. As it was believed that the Indians would be less on their guard just before dawn than at any other hour of the night, the line of march was not to be taken up until two o'clock in the morning. At that hour the great gate of the fort was thrown open and the selected troops, two hundred and fifty in number, filed silently out into the intense darkness of the sultry night.

In close order and without the utterance of a word they marched up the river road, the black waters gleaming dimly on their right. Their left was bounded by the white houses of Canadian settlers, with their barns and orchards and cornfields. From these they were saluted by the clamorous barking of watch-dogs, while many a startled face peered anxiously at them from the unshuttered windows. The frightened inhabitants, roused from sleep by the unusual sound of marching troops, were filled with uneasiness, and gathered in little groups by the roadside to question each other and listen to the measured tramping as it was borne faintly back to them on the damp night air.

Besides these there were other figures flitting behind the houses, through the rustling cornfields and from tree to tree of the orchards, as still and dark as shadows, but ever keeping pace with the marching troops, and ever watching them. These were the scouts of Pontiac, without whose knowledge no man had left the gates of Detroit by day or night for more than a year. Out on the water was heard the muffled sound of oars from the two bateaux, each armed with a swivel gun that kept abreast of the troops close to the river bank.

Nearly two miles from the fort, Parent's creek, ever since that memorable night called "Bloody Run," crossed the road at right angles through a rough ravine, and entered the river a short distance below amid a rank growth of sedge and wild rice. It was spanned by a rude wooden bridge and beyond this the bank rose steeply. On its summit were piled stacks of firewood provided for winter's use by the thrifty Canadians; while from it stretched away another series of orchards and fields, enclosed by stout fences. As the dark column of troops struck the bridge, its hollow echoes rang ominously in their ears and a deadly chill seemed to come into the air.

The advanced guard had crossed the bridge and breasted the steep ascent to its summit. The narrow structure behind them was choked by the passage of the main body. All were pressing eagerly forward, anxious to gain the open ground beyond; when suddenly there arose, clear and shrill from the blackness beside them, the terrible war-cry of Pontiac. It was instantly answered by a burst of yells and a blaze of fire from every wood-pile, fence, and tree, behind which the fierce Ottawa warriors had been concealed for hours in anticipation of this moment.

Before that withering fire the advanced guard, leaving half their number dead behind them, staggered back on the main body, and all recoiled together. The little bridge became clogged beyond its capacity with panic-stricken humanity, those in front striving to fly, those in the rear endeavoring to advance, until dozens of dead, wounded, and even of those untouched by bullet were forced over the unrailed sides into the gloomy depths below. If at this moment an attack had been made from the rear, not a man of Dalzell's force would ever have regained Fort Detroit. This was what Pontiac had planned, and, for want of allies whom he could more fully trust, he had consigned this important duty to Mahng and his Ojibwas. Now, amid the roar of battle, he listened with strained ears for the firing that should denote the Ojibwa attack. But no sound came from that direction, and the heart of the great warrior sank within him as he realized that a vital part of his plan had miscarried.

He had scant time for reflection, however, for the brave Dalzell, forcing his way to the front, raised his cheery voice with encouraging shouts, rallied his bewildered men, and led them on a fierce charge up the heights. One more crashing volley was poured into their ranks, but it no longer came as a surprise, and mad with fury the redcoats swept on to the summit. To their amazement, it was as deserted as though no human being had ever trodden its soil. The place from which, a moment before, Indian guns had flashed in their faces, was as silent as the grave. The enemy had vanished in the blackness as though by magic, and unaccustomed to the tactics of forest warfare, the newly arrived troops became filled with a mysterious fear.

Still their leader urged them forward, and the uncertain march was continued for a short distance until it became apparent that the fence lines had been changed, so as to lead them from the road, and that they were involved in a maze of outbuildings and enclosures. As they blindly groped their way, starting nervously at every contact with each other, and becoming each moment more confused, the shrill war-cry was again raised, in their very ears; the guns of an unseen foe again flashed in their faces, and they were furiously attacked from all sides at once. They could not fight back; for if they sprang at the flash of a gun, it was only to find an empty space. A cry arose that they were being surrounded, and in another minute the whole force was in a panic-stricken retreat, rushing pell-mell down the bank and across the bridge which was still held by the rear guard under Captain Grant.

Here Dalzell managed to restore partial order and give his men a certain degree of confidence by ordering the crews of the bateaux, which had come up the creek, to sweep the opposite bank with grape from their swivel guns. Thus the enemy was held in check while such of the wounded as could be found were got into the boats. The moment this task was accomplished the retreat was resumed, while the Indians sprang in pursuit, pouring in a heavy fire from the rear and both flanks. Every now and then the rear guard faced about and delivered a volley at their yelling pursuers, who promptly returned it with interest. Still the way was open to the fort, and no serious fears were entertained that this would not eventually be reached, until, when half the distance was covered, the main body came opposite to a newly dug cellar. In this were concealed a strong force of Indians under Pontiac himself, who had hurried them to this point with the hope of still cutting off the retreat, and making good the previous failure of his plan. The advance was allowed to pass. Then came again the terrible signal-cry of the Ottawa chieftain. With it his warriors delivered such an unexpected and scathing volley that the bewildered troops again broke ranks, and, not knowing which way to fly, huddled together like sheep in their frenzied efforts to escape the hail of bullets.

Dalzell, already twice wounded, threatened his men, pleaded with them, beat them into line with the flat of his sword, and finally rallied them in a charge that cleared the fatal cellar of its yelling inmates. But the moment the retreat was resumed the attack became as fierce and galling as ever. Pontiac distributed his warriors from house to house, stationing them in such advantageous positions that their fire was well-nigh unsupportable, and every rod of the road to safety must be stubbornly contested.

It was now daylight, and through the morning mist the harassed soldiers could see their agile foes darting forward to cut off stragglers, despatch the wounded, or scalp the dead, leaping back, firing, and running to new positions, all the time yelling like so many demons. A strong party opening fire from behind a range of fences, Captain Gray was ordered to dislodge them. He obeyed, and fell mortally wounded at the head of his charging company. The moment his men turned their backs, the active foe rushed to their old position, and their fire became hotter than before.

The retreat was now resolved into a flight, the dead lay where they fell, and the wounded were abandoned to their fate. A sergeant shot through the hips raised himself on his hands and gazed despairingly after the retiring battalion. Dalzell saw him. They had fought together on many a stubborn field, and the commander could not leave his old comrade to perish. He sprang to the rescue of the wounded man, and was lifting him when struck and instantly killed by an Indian bullet. Few saw him fall, and none dared attempt the recovery of his body.

With the death of their gallant leader, the retreating troops became a panic-stricken mob in which every one looked out for himself. Only Grant's little company and Rogers' handful of rangers stood firm, and by occupying house after house as they slowly fell back, protected somewhat the flight of the main body.

The exhausted fugitives were still at a distance from the fort when they were met by an irregular company of traders and their employees, the sole force that Gladwyn dared spare from his slender garrison, under command of Paymaster Bullen. The little man in buckskin displayed such coolness and good judgment, and was so ably supported by his motley following, that from that moment the disastrous retreat was effectively covered. By eight o'clock, or after six hours of marching and fighting, the disorganized remnant of the little army, that had set forth to wipe Pontiac and his red followers from the face of the earth, found themselves, as by a miracle, once more behind the sheltering palisades of the fort, which for many months thereafter they had no desire to leave.

About this time, the Ottawa chieftain who had won this signal victory, returned to his village with so moody a brow, that even his own followers durst not utter their rejoicings in his presence. He had been so confident of destroying Dalzell's entire force and his plans had been so well laid, that to have them miscarry through treachery, aroused his utmost fury. Thus he now proposed to deal with the traitors in such a manner that there would be no chance of their example becoming contagious among the warriors who still acknowledged his authority.

CHAPTER XXXVI
BRAVE DEATH OF THE OLD MAJOR

The evening preceding that night of death and terror was spent quietly and pleasantly, as was their wont, by Edith and Ah-mo in Major Hester's room. It was an unusually happy time, for Ah-mo, having received her father's permission to do so, told them of Donald, his bravery, his wounds, his captivity, the strange manner in which he had been identified by the mark of a totem on his arm, his recovery from illness in the secluded quiet of Pontiac's island, and the glad tidings that, on the morrow, he would be allowed to visit them.

To both Major Hester and Edith the first knowledge that Donald was a prisoner came as a shock, but when they reflected upon the kindness with which they had been treated, and realized, from Ah-mo's account, that the young ensign was regarded with equal favor by Pontiac, they became reconciled to the idea of his captivity, and only anxious to note for themselves his reported recovery from the illness caused by wounds. So they impatiently watched the passing of the hours that brought him nearer to them, and beguiled the time by talking of him. Major Hester told the story of Songa and Mahng, and how the life of the former had been saved by the baby Donald. With infinite zest he recalled the kick with which he had repelled Mahng's attack on the young Ottawa chief, who was now known to all men as Pontiac.

Ah-mo had never before heard of this, and she anxiously wondered if that Mahng could be the same who was now the leader of one of the Ojibwa bands.

But the major was still reminiscing, and describing the brave deed of Songa's beautiful squaw.

"My mother," murmured Ah-mo.

"And more worthy of honor than a queen!" exclaimed the major.

Then he told of their escape from Tawtry House, of Donald's subsequent disappearance, and of the strange mark found on his arm when he was restored to them.

"I soon learned," said the old soldier, "that it was the symbol of a totem, though

I never knew why it was tattooed on the child's arm, nor by whom. Perhaps you can tell us of it, Ah-mo. It was something after this fashion."

Here the major drew a sketch of the design on a bit of paper.

"Yes," replied the Indian girl, regarding the sketch, "from this alone could I tell the clan of the warrior wearing it, his standing in the tribe, and who had tattooed the symbol. Even without the sketch I could have told you these things, for I have looked upon the original."

"When?" asked Edith, wonderingly.

"At the time when my father recognized his own handiwork on the arm of a captive."

"You then have seen our Donald and never told us of the meeting, nor what he said, nor anything!" exclaimed the white girl, in a grieved tone.

"I have seen him twice," replied Ah-mo, "but we have never exchanged words, nor do I think he knows who I am. The first time I saw him was shortly after my coming from Montreal, when I was on the river in a canoe with one of my girl friends. He was also in a canoe, but helplessly drifting, having broken his only paddle. I laughed at his predicament and would have let him drift, had not my companion mentioned his name. It was one esteemed by all of Indian blood, and though I knew not whether the young man bore any relation to my father's friend, I determined, for the sake of his name, to help him. We approached him so quietly that he did not hear us, tossed a paddle into his canoe, and were off almost before he knew of our presence. That was one time. The other was but a few weeks since, when I stood with my father and a captive was laid unconscious at our feet. My father knew him not, and but for the totem would never have recognized him."

"What is this totem?" inquired Edith.

"It is that of the Bear, the same to which my father belongs."

"And you, too, and your brothers?"

"No, we belong to our mother's totem, which is that of the Beaver, for no one may belong to the totem of his father."

"And what means the circle of serpents?" asked Major Hester.

"It signifies the magic circle of the Metai, to which none but a brave warrior, who has won the honor by some notable deed, may belong."

"But Donald was a child."

"Was he not by birth a warrior who could be naught but brave? and had he not already, as you have just told, saved the life of a chief of the Metai?" queried Ah-mo.

"True, so he had," asserted the major. "But what is this Metai of which you speak?"

"Being a woman, I know but little of it," answered the Indian girl. "It is a powerful order of much mystery extending over many tribes. It is greatly feared by those who do not belong to it, while those who do will aid each other in any extremity and to the full extent of their powers. In it are many degrees of merit, and he who is its chief must be obeyed by all who acknowledge its authority."

"Why, girl, you are describing free-masonry!" cried the major, who was himself a master-mason. "Have the members of this Metai signs and passwords by which they may recognize each other?"

"They have, but I know them not," replied Ah-mo.

"Of course not, seeing that you are a girl; but Pontiac is certain to know something of this thing, and, if the mighty brotherhood that encircles the world has indeed penetrated the American wilderness, then will we settle this useless war in short order. By the way, Ah-mo, who is the present chief of this magic circle? or is it not known to the uninitiated?"

"It is known to all who care to know," replied the girl, proudly, "for his name is Pontiac, and it is his own mark, which no other may use, that encloses the all-seeing eye of the Metai on your son's arm."

"Whew-w-w," whistled the major, reflectingly. "So that is the secret of Pontiac's wide-spread influence? Well, I must see and question him about it to-morrow. Now, girls, leave me, for it is late, and Ah-mo's revelations have given me much food for thought."

As he kissed his daughter good-night and blessed her, so he also, for the first time, kissed Ah-mo and gave her his blessing, saying that she was becoming as dear to him as an own daughter.

As the two girls crossed the space intervening between Major Hester's quarters and the house in which they slept, Edith wondered that they did not meet any of the guards who were generally so quick to note every movement in that vicinity, especially at night. She was also impressed with Ah-mo's unusual silence and her frequent starts at the little noises made by birds or insects. When they reached their room, the Indian girl sat by the open window, saying that she did not feel like going to bed just yet, and after a while Edith fell asleep leaving her sitting gazing out into the night.

It seemed many hours later when she awoke to find her companion still sitting in the same position. On rising and going to her, she found the Indian girl to be trembling as though with a chill.

"What is it, Ah-mo?" she asked in alarm. "Are you ill, dear?"

As though in answer there came a roar of musketry from a point not far distant, and yells, and shrill cries, and the sharp crack of rifles.

At the sounds Pontiac's daughter sprang up, crying: "It has begun! Oh, my father! my father!"

"What does it mean? Tell me, Ah-mo!" gasped Edith, her voice sunk to a whisper with terror.

"It is a battle," replied the Indian girl, sternly, "between thy people and my people. It is time to dress and be prepared for what may happen."

In a few minutes Edith, fully dressed, declared that she must go to her father, that they might share together whatever danger threatened.

"Whither you go," replied the other, "there must I go also," and so they left the house in company. They heard the old Canadian couple who owned it moving about as they went out, but did not stop to speak to them. As they gained the road, the firing, which had been momentarily silenced, broke out afresh apparently nearer than before. In Major Hester's quarters they saw a dim light, and with clasped hands they started to run toward it.

At that moment a score of dark figures appeared, coming swiftly from the direction of the light. The next instant the girls were surrounded, seized in brawny arms, and borne away, their gasping cries of terror being smothered ere they were fully uttered.

An hour later, in the gray of dawn, two young men came hurrying down the road. "Is that the place, Atoka?" asked one, pointing to the house occupied by Major Hester, in front of which a little group of frightened Canadian peasants were gathered.

His companion nodded assent, whereupon the other exclaimed, "Thank God, there has been no fighting here!" Then he sprang forward, scattering the Canadians, who recoiled in terror at his sudden appearance, and entered the house. In another minute a bitter cry rang from the open windows, and the hearers crossed themselves at the sound.

Donald Hester had discovered his father lying in a pool of blood, from which none had dared lift him, and pierced by a dozen wounds, but still breathing.

"Father! Dear father! Speak to me. It is your own boy, Donald!" cried the youth in pitiful accents, as he raised the prostrate form in his arms. "Tell me, father, who has done this thing."

The dying man opened his eyes, and fixed them full on the face of his son. For a few seconds he gazed on the loved features, and his lips moved as in a blessing, though no sound came from them. Then, with a smile of ineffable sweetness, and a sigh of perfect content, the light faded from the dear eyes, and the spirit of the brave old soldier passed gently from the war-worn body into the fadeless dawn of eternity.

Very tenderly did Donald lift the lifeless body of his father to the humble pallet that had been the soldier's bed for many weeks. Then he sat beside it, keeping motionless watch over his dead, while Atoka stood silently in the doorway guarding the grief of his friend from curious intrusion.

CHAPTER XXXVII
THE CURSE OF THE MAGIC CIRCLE

From the moment that Donald Hester's brave shout of warning saved the schooner from capture, he was like one who sleeps, until he awoke to consciousness amid the strange surroundings of an Indian lodge. Soft hands were bathing his throbbing brow, and when he opened his eyes they rested on a face of such loveliness, and at the same time so filled with pity, that it seemed to him but the fairest fragment of a beautiful dream. The radiant smile that greeted his restoration to life gave the face a strangely familiar look; but he was too weak to remember where he had seen it, and fell asleep from the weariness of the effort. When he next awoke he was much stronger, and gazed eagerly about with the hope that the face might prove a reality; but nowhere could he discover it, nor did it appear to him again.

He was devotedly cared for by an old squaw, the most skilled nurse in all the Ottawa tribe, and by a young warrior whom he came to know as Atoka. Others occasionally visited the lodge, but never the one he longed to see, and so he finally decided that the face had indeed come to him in a dream and not in reality.

Aided by youth and the magic of Indian simples, Donald's recovery was certain and rapid. Atoka was his constant companion, and, to while away the slow hours, each taught the other his own language. One day the Indian lad made mention of his sister Ah-mo, and Donald caught eagerly at the name. At once it was connected with his vision and with a long ago day of sunshine on the river.

"Is she not the daughter of Pontiac?" he inquired.

"Yes."

"Then you must be a son of the great chief?"

"I am his son," replied the young Indian, proudly.

"Am I, then, Pontiac's prisoner?"

"No. One bearing the sign of the Metai may be Pontiac's guest, but never his prisoner."

"Ah, yes! I forgot my symbolic marking. But tell me, Atoka, was not your sister with two white women on an island not long since?"

"She was. But they were taken to Detroit in exchange for prisoners held in the fort."

In saying this Atoka believed he was telling the truth, for he knew not that Edith still remained in the Ottawa village. From the day that Donald was placed in his charge he had not left the island, nor had any of its other occupants, save occasionally to hunt or fish, for Pontiac did not wish it generally known that a white captive was held there.

As the means of intelligent intercourse between the young men increased, Donald learned many other things of which he had been ignorant, and among them that his own father was also a prisoner, or, as Atoka said, a guest, in the Ottawa village.

"When you have recovered your full strength, then am I to take you to him, for so Pontiac has ordered," added Atoka.

Thus inspired to gain strength, Donald did so with such rapidity that, a week later, he was able to throw Atoka in a wrestling match, and the young warrior sent word to his father that he should bring his charge to the village on the following day.

Donald was so excited at the prospect of a near reunion with his beloved parent, that, to his impatience, no hours had ever seemed so long as did those of that last day of his seclusion. He retired early in order to shorten them by sleep, but was wide awake when startled by the sound of distant, though heavy and continuous firing.

"It is an attack on the Ottawa village," he said.

"Or on the fort," answered Atoka.

Both were so impatient to visit the scene of conflict that neither needed to be reminded of their purpose to go to the village on that very day. So in a few minutes they had launched a canoe and set forth, with what results, we have already learned.

As Donald watched beside his father's body, a hand was laid on his shoulder, and one whom he recognized as Pontiac stood beside him, his stern face softened by sorrow.

"He was my friend," said the chieftain. "I loved him with a love that was more than that of a brother. Now that he has gone, night has fallen, and all things are hidden in darkness. Long years ago he saved my life, and in so doing made an enemy of him who has now taken his in revenge. This man is a dog of dogs, and from this hour he is outcast among the children of the forest. With the curse of the Metai shall he be cursed, he and his forever. I, Pontiac, Chief of the Magic Circle, have said it."

"What is his name, and where may he be found?" asked Donald, eagerly.

"His name is Mahng, and he is of the Ojibwas, though where he may be found I know not yet. But found he must be, for not only is he the murderer of thy father and my friend, and a traitor to all in whose veins runs Indian blood, but he has stolen and taken with him those most dear to thee and to me, thy sister and my daughter."

"What!" cried Donald, springing to his feet. "My sister, say you? Is she not safe in the fort?"

"No," answered Pontiac, sadly. "For safety did I keep her here, with her father. Now is she gone, and with her is gone Ah-mo, my daughter, and my right hand.

To recover them, and to avenge this death, I might command the Ottawa nation to follow me, and they would obey. I might destroy the Ojibwas from the face of the earth, but it may not be. In a private quarrel I may not array tribe against tribe. Nor in this case would the strength of a war-party prove of such value as the cunning of two men. The one is doubtless expected, and will be watched for, while the others may pass unnoticed. Therefore have I selected two who shall be intrusted with this mission and vengeance. They are my two sons, one of whom is of the Totem of the Bear, and the other of the Totem of the Beaver, so that two totems shall be matched against one, for Mahng is of the Totem of the Wolf. One of them is, besides, of the order of Metai, on which Mahng has no claim."

"But am I not to be allowed to take part in the rescue of my own sister? Am I to be kept here, a miserable captive, while others do the work that is rightly mine?" cried Donald.

"My son," replied Pontiac, again laying his hand gently on the young man's shoulder, "art thou not of the order of the Metai, and of my totem, the Totem of the Bear? Hast thou not been the son of my heart from the day thy baby arms clasped my neck and saved me from death? I had no thought but that thou should go as one of my messengers, and Atoka shall go with thee."

So it was planned in that chamber of death. After a while four venerable warriors, all of the Metai, were summoned; Atoka, who had as yet performed no deed to entitle him to membership, was sent outside to guard the door; and, in the presence of his dead father, Donald Hester was initiated into the dread secrets of the magic circle. It was a solemn and trying ordeal, and his face was very pale when it was ended; but his mouth was firm-set and he seemed to have gained in manliness of bearing.

A few hours later the body of Major Hester, wrapped in the flag he had served so faithfully, was laid to rest in the presence of a thousand Indians, whose friend he had ever been, and over his grave a file of Ottawa warriors fired the echoing volley that betokened their respect for his rank.

Then was Donald led away to Pontiac's own lodge, where, in pursuance of the plan already formed, his entire body was stained a rich coppery brown and he was, in other ways, carefully disguised as an Ottawa warrior. It was given out that Atoka was to be sent as a runner to announce Pontiac's recent victory to distant tribes and

At War with Pontiac

to solicit their aid in carrying on the war. It was also whispered that he was to be accompanied by a member of the Metai, who should proclaim the dread curse of the magic circle against Mahng, the Ojibwa, and all who should give him aid. As the proceedings of this mysterious order were always conducted in secret, no one was surprised that the identity of its messenger was not disclosed, nor that his departure should be made at night unseen of all men save only Pontiac, chief of the Metai.

So greatly did Mahng dread the wrath of Pontiac, that from the first he took every precaution to conceal the traces of his flight. Thus Donald was obliged to set forth on this renewed search for his lost sister without an idea of what course to pursue. He only knew that the country of the Ojibwas lay to the north, and so in this direction were his steps first directed.

For many weeks did he and Atoka travel by land and over the waters of the Great Lakes, down swift rushing streams, along dim trails and through weary leagues of pathless forest, where they were only guided by that instinct of woodcraft which, in an Indian, ranks with the keenest of his senses. To Saginaw and Thunder Bay they went, to Michilimackinac and L'abre Croche, even to the far northern Sault of Ste. Marie, without finding those whom they sought. In every Indian village and camp, in every forest lodge, and to the lone hunter, whenever they crossed his trail, did they proclaim the dread message of the Metai by which Mahng, the Ojibwa, was outcast forever.

The uninitiated listened with fear and trembling; but everywhere they found brave warriors and stately chiefs, who gave the answer of the magic circle:--

".," and did everything possible to speed their errand.

In all this time they found no sign, nor until they began to retrace their steps did they gain tidings of their quest. Now, here and there, they began to come across trembling wretches who had been with Mahng on that fatal night, but whom the terrible, far-reaching curse had since driven terror-stricken from him. Of these they learned that he had, from the first, made his way to the south to the country of the Shawnees, who had at first received him kindly. Then, as the dread sentence of the Metai reached those remoter parts, he was driven from camp to camp until there was none who dared give him shelter or aid. So he turned to the far west with a purpose of joining the fierce Dacotahs beyond the great river.

Following this faint clue, Donald and Atoka crossed Lake Michigan, ascended

Green bay and the swift waters of the Fox until they could portage into the wide torrent of the Wisconsin. This they purposed to descend to the Mississippi, on whose banks they hoped for further news.

One day in the late autumn they came to a place where they must needs carry around a great fall, the roar of whose plunging waters could be heard for miles through the silent forest. From their landing Donald entered the narrow trail of the carry first, bearing the canoe on his head and shoulders, while Atoka followed after a slight delay, with their rifles and scanty camp equipage. At the highest point of the carry the pathway, barely wide enough for the passage of two persons, skirted the very brink of the awful precipice over which thundered the cataract.

Here Donald came suddenly face to face with a slight figure, bending beneath a burden, whom he instantly recognized as Ah-mo, the daughter of Pontiac. At the same moment a man emerged from behind a point of rock a few paces beyond her, whom Donald knew by instinct to be Mahng. Hurling his burden from him, careless of its fate, and shouting the anathema of the Metai, the avenger sprang past the crouching girl to grapple with his mortal foe. But the latter did not await him. With the terrible words he had so long dreaded to hear ringing in his ears, he turned to fly, slipped on the wet rocks, clutched wildly at the empty air, and pitched headlong into the awful depths of the seething caldron a hundred feet below.

CHAPTER XXXVIII
A WINTER IN THE WILDERNESS

For a moment Donald stood rooted to the spot by the suddenness and awfulness of the fate that had overtaken his enemy. Then like a flash it came to him that, even while his attention was wholly centred on the tragedy just enacted, he had been aware of another man ascending the pathway who had turned and fled. Was he then to be robbed of the fruits of his arduous journeyings? Was Edith again to be snatched from him when almost within his reach? No, not if he, alone and unarmed, were forced to battle for her with a score of Mahng's treacherous followers. So thinking, he sprang down the steep trail with a reckless disregard of everything save the necessity of gaining its further end with all possible speed.

Less than a minute had elapsed since he first caught sight of Mahng. In two more he reached the end of the trail beside a pool of dark water only to find the place untenanted. Out in the river, still within rifle-shot, but speeding down stream as though in deadly fear, was a single canoe in which were three persons. Donald felt certain that two of these were females. Of course one was Edith, and though yet within sight, she was as hopelessly removed from him as though they were separated by leagues instead of rods. His own canoe had gone over the precipice, there was no trail through the dense forest growth that overhung the river bank, and if there were he could hardly have kept pace with that fleeting shadow out in the swift current. Yes, Edith was again lost to him, and as the now distant canoe rounded a bend and vanished from his sight, the young man threw himself on the ground, overcome by a dumb despair.

From this state he was roused by the sound of footsteps, and of a soft voice saying, "Donald Hester." He sprang to his feet to find Ah-mo and Atoka standing before him. The former was thin and worn as though with weariness and anxiety, and, though her face was now lighted by the radiance of a transition from despair to a new hope, much of its former beauty was wanting. She was holding out a hand and saying:--

"Donald Hester, I did not know who you were until Atoka came and told me. But I did know that you saved my life, for so great was my misery and despair that in another minute I should have ended both by an act that I now shudder to recall. So I thank you, Donald Hester, who art now become my brother, since Pontiac claims you for a son."

"I did nothing worthy of thanks, Ah-mo, my sister," answered Donald, bitterly, "and now that Edith is again lost to me, I feel that I have done worse than nothing. But tell me of her. Is she well? and what treatment does she receive at the hands of Mahng's ruffians?"

"I know not," replied Ah-mo, sadly, "for it is now many weeks since we were cruelly separated, and whither she was taken I have no knowledge."

"What?" cried Donald, "was she not with you on this very spot but a few minutes since? and did I not see her borne despairingly away in a canoe that is but just lost to sight?"

"No, there was none with me save Mahng and his brother and their wives. We have travelled long and wearily since Edith was torn from my arms, and of her fate I know nothing. I was being taken to the north that I might marry Suggema, the son of Mahng, who believed that my father would thus be compelled to withdraw his curse."

"And did you wish for this marriage?" asked Donald, curiously.

"Did I not say that I was on the point of throwing myself from yonder cliff to escape the misery of such a thing?"

"Forgive me, my sister," said the young man, humbly. "I had no cause to doubt you, nor do I. It was a thoughtless question."

With their mission thus partly fulfilled, Donald and Atoka were confronted by the serious problem of what move to make next. The season was nearing winter. In a short time the streams would be frozen, and the forest trails choked with snow. They had no canoe and it was too late in the year to peel bark with which to construct one. Their supply of food was scanty, and very soon the game on which they were wholly dependent would disappear from that part of the country. Then, too, Ah-mo's strength was so nearly spent that she was in no condition for rough travel, even had they the means to go and a knowledge of what direction to take. So, after a long discussion, it was reluctantly decided that they must remain where they were until the coming of spring with its flowing sap should enable them to build another canoe, and resume their search for Donald's sister.

The succeeding weeks were filled with busy and arduous toil. A winter in that latitude, where the mercury often falls to 20 degrees and even 30 degrees below zero, can only be successfully encountered after elaborate preparation, and the little company who now found themselves stranded on the verge of that vast northern forest, had everything to do, with but slight means and scanty time. The followers of Mahng had abandoned many things in their hasty flight which now proved of the utmost value, and a welcome addition to the limited outfit of Donald and Atoka. Among these things were several blankets, an axe, and a few rude cooking-utensils.

These they removed to the spot selected for their winter home, about a mile from the river on the bank of a small stream that flowed into it and near by a pond formed by an old and very large beaver dam. Here, before night of that first day, a snug hut of bark was erected for Ah-mo's accommodation, and from here the young men set forth the next morning on the busiest season of hunting and trapping in which either of them had ever engaged. Everything that wore fur or feathers and could furnish meat to be smoked or dried for future use was eagerly sought. Their success was phenomenal. Deer, bear, turkeys, and geese fell before their rifles, while their traps, in the construction of which Atoka was a past-master, yielded beaver, otter, muskrat, and raccoons.

Within a month they had collected such a quantity of meat and skins as assured them against both hunger and cold between then and spring. Now they turned their attention to a house, and, with only their ready axes for tools, they had one finished two weeks later that they surveyed with genuine pleasure and pardonable pride. It was of logs, notched and fitted together at the corners, twelve feet square and with walls six feet high. It was chinked with moss, had a tight floor of hewed cedar planks, a roof of hemlock bark, a chimney and fireplace of stones cemented with blue clay and sand, two small windows covered with scraped and tightly stretched intestines taken from a deer, and a stout door hung on wooden hinges.

The hut was hardly ready for occupancy before the winter storms set in and the whole forest world was buried in snow. Still the inmates of "Castle Beaver," as Donald named their cosy dwelling, were by no means idle nor did an hour of time hang heavily on their hands for lack of occupation. Ah-mo had gathered an immense supply of flags and sedge grass, from which she not only braided enough of the matting, so commonly used among the northern tribes, to enclose her own corner of the hut, but to cover all the interior walls as well. The floor was warmly spread with skins, from which their couches were also formed.

Besides always adding to the comforts of their home, they found plenty of indoor work in the way of cutting out buckskin and fur garments which were sewed with deer sinew, the making of snowshoes and wooden bowls, and the braiding of mats. For recreation Donald told tales of the great world beyond the sea, Ah-mo related incidents of her life in Montreal, and Atoka recalled many a weird Indian legend. They also played simple games. Atoka was taught to read and write from copies set by Donald, while all three improved their knowledge of English, French, and several Indian dialects. For outside work there were traps to be visited, snow to be cleared from the path leading to the river, the water hole through the ice to be chopped out every day, water to be fetched, wood to be cut for the roaring fireplace, fish to be caught through the ice in the pond, and an occasional hunt to be taken after fresh meat.

In all this busy life Ah-mo, who had fully recovered her strength and beauty, was ever the leading spirit. At the same time she was so modest and intelligent, so cheerful and uncomplaining, that Donald regarded her with ever-increasing respect and admiration.

"If Edith were only with us," he would sigh, "I think I should be content to dwell here for the rest of my life," whereat Ah-mo would laugh and bid him be cautious how he made such rash statements. Never a day passed but what they talked of Edith and planned their search for her. Donald, too, often spoke of his dear friend Christie, who, he declared, was the one white man of his acquaintance with whom he would be willing to share this pleasant forest life.

At length the winter came to an end. The south winds began to blow, the snow to melt, the ice to break up, the wild geese to fly northward in V-shaped companies, and the sap to run in the trees. While the snow was still on the ground, they gathered sap from the rock maples and boiled it into a plentiful supply of sugar. After that came the building of a canoe and the fashioning of its paddles.

It was with high hopes, but at the same time with genuine regret, that, late in May, they bade farewell to their winter home, launched a canoe, deep-laden with their accumulated stock of furs, and started southward on the swift waters of the Wisconsin. For weeks they floated with its current, and on the mighty volume of the Mississippi. At the newly established trading-post of St. Louis they exchanged their furs for ammunition and such goods as they needed, but at such extortionate rates as made Donald's blood boil with anger.

Here, for the first time in many months, they met white men, but none of these suspected for a moment that Donald was aught but the Indian he appeared, nor did he undeceive them, and after a short stay their journey was resumed. It was still southward to the Ohio, then up that river and the Wabash to the place where Ah-mo and Edith had been separated. Here, with all their efforts, they could only learn that the white girl had been taken to the eastward into the country of the Delawares. So they patiently retraced their course down the winding Wabash, and then continued their way up the Ohio to the Scioto and the Muskingum, stopping to make inquiries at every Indian camp and village through all that vast territory.

Sometimes they seemed to find a clue, but it was always quickly lost, and toward the end of the summer they were well-nigh despairing. Only Ah-mo remained cheerfully hopeful and ever urged the others to fresh efforts.

At length, in September, they learned the startling news that a great English army was descending the Ohio from Fort Pitt, and that its commander, Colonel Bouquet, had summoned all the Indians of that region to meet him on the Muskingum. There they were to deliver to him every white captive whom they held and sign a treaty of peace, or else he would ravage their country with fire and bullet. From the moment he heard of this Donald determined to attend that great gathering, and his companions willingly consented to accompany him.

CHAPTER XXXIX
AN ADOPTED DAUGHTER OF THE FOREST

So forgetful had the people of Pennsylvania become of the example of their great founder that they systematically robbed, cheated, and murdered the unfortunate Indians with whom they had dealings, until, fired by the eloquence of Pontiac, these rose in rebellion and began a fierce war of revenge. Now the panic-stricken traders and frontier settlers, who were directly responsible for this state of affairs, demanded that a bounty be offered for Indian scalps. By their clamor they at length forced the English governor of the colony to yield to their demands and sign the infamous bill. It provided that a reward averaging one hundred dollars be paid for the scalp of every Indian, man, woman, or child, killed within the limits of the province. Upon the issuing of this proclamation, to quote a leading historian, "an era of carnage ensued, during which the worst acts of Indian ferocity were thrown into the shade by the enormities of white barbarians."

Dwelling in a Shawnee village at this time was an English soldier named David Owens, who had deserted from Braddock's army ten years before and joined the Indians. He had been kindly received, adopted into the tribe, had married the daughter of a chief, and become the father of two children. With the prospect of gaining a reward for Indian scalps, all the cupidity of this man's fiendish nature was aroused, and on the approach of Bouquet's army he conceived a plan for enriching himself and at the same time escaping the punishment due him as a deserter. While meditating it he found himself encamped one night with two warriors, his own wife, another woman, and his two children. Toward morning he arose, and seeing by the dim light of the camp-fire that the others were buried in profound sleep, he placed two rifles so that their muzzles were close to the heads of the unconscious warriors and pulled both triggers at the same instant. Then, with hatchet and knife, he deliberately despatched the women and children, who cowered about him in helpless terror. With the horrible evidences of his crime dangling from his belt he then set forth for the nearest English outpost. Here he was not only paid for his scalps, but pardoned for his desertion and given a commission as interpreter in Bouquet's army.

So infuriated were the inmates of the village to which the victims of this outrage belonged, that, in retaliation, they determined to put to death six white captives who happened to be in their power. These were to be tortured on so many successive days. Five of them suffered their dreadful fate before the eyes of the sixth, and, at length, it came his turn to be led to the stake. He was a stalwart, handsome fellow, who had been held as a slave for more than a year. He had refused several offers of adoption, preferring to retain the privilege of effecting an escape, if he could, to pledging his loyalty to the tribe. So, as a slave, he had been made to toil early and late for his savage masters. Now, having fruitlessly exhausted every means of escape, as well as his powers of pleading for his own life, he determined to meet his fate as bravely as became a British soldier. With a rope about his neck, and a face betraying no trace of the horror and despair that filled his soul, he walked calmly through the jeering throng of spectators to the fatal stake.

The rope was already made fast to it, and the signal for the first act of the dreadful drama was about to be given, when a fair-haired girl, mounted on a pony, dashed through the crowd, scattering it to right and left. She severed the rope that bound the motionless captive to the tree of death, and then, wheeling about, delivered, with flashing eyes and bitter tongue, a harangue in the Indian language that caused her hearers to hang their heads in shame. She termed them cowards for visiting their vengeance on innocent and helpless captives, and fearlessly bade them begone from her sight, ere she called down the wrath of the Great Spirit on their heads.

As the abashed savages slunk away before the sting of her burning words, the girl, trembling with excitement, slid from her pony's back to the ground. Instantly the strong arm of him whom she had rescued was offered for her support, and she was electrified by the sound of her own name, which she had not heard for many months.

"I thank you, Edith Hester, for my life," said the young man, simply.

For a moment she stared at him bewildered. Then, with a flash of recognition, she answered:--

"And I thank God that he has granted me the privilege of saving it, James Christie."

When Edith was borne away captive by Mahng, the Ojibwa, he maliciously told her of her father's death and that her brother had also been killed by Pontiac's express order. Having burdened himself with this prisoner, on the impulse of the moment, Mahng was soon embarrassed as to how he should dispose of her. He dared not kill her, for he contemplated seeking an alliance with the English. At the same time, she proved a decided encumbrance on his rapid journeyings. Thus when he discovered that the wife of Custaloga, a Shawnee chief, who had recently lost her only daughter, was willing to adopt Edith in her place, he gladly relinquished his fair prisoner.

Custaloga and his wife and his sons were so proud of the beautiful white girl, whom they now claimed as daughter and sister, and treated her with such unvarying kindness that before long she became really attached to them. As she reflected that with her own father and brother dead, her former life had no longer a claim on her, she grew reconciled to that of the forest, and determined to make the best of her situation. So she devoted herself to learning the language of her new people, and before long, by her fearlessness and strength of character, coupled with many acts of kindness, gained a decided influence over them.

She was always a friend of the white captives among the Shawnees and succeeded in lightening many of their burdens. At length, while on a journey with her adopted mother and youngest brother, she heard of the terrible tragedy even then being enacted in a Shawnee village only a few miles from where they were encamped. Fired with horror and pity, she impulsively sprang on her pony and dashed away in the direction of the village, which she reached just in time to save the life of James Christie.

Ere she left the village, she obtained a pledge from the warriors of that band that his life should not again be endangered at their hands, and that in the future he should be well treated. Then, promising to see him again when they should come back that way, Edith bade the young soldier farewell and returned to the lodge that was now her home. From that moment she was conscious of a change in her feelings, and of a longing for the life of her own people which was already beginning to seem strange and remote.

It so happened that Edith and Christie did not meet again until at the great gathering of the Ohio valley Indians and their captives, held on the banks of the beautiful Muskingum by order of Colonel Bouquet. Edith was brought in first, and though she protested that she had no desire to leave her adopted parents, she was so warmly welcomed by the commander and his officers, many of whom had known both her father and brother, that she gradually allowed herself to be persuaded to a renewed trial of civilization. So strange seemed the dress with which she was provided by the matrons, who accompanied the expedition for the express purpose of caring for the female captives, that for days she would only consent to wear it for an hour or so at a time.

All this while there was daily witnessed in Bouquet's camp some of the most pathetic scenes of that strange war, the bringing in of hundreds of captives of both sexes and all ages, and the eager search among them of husbands, brothers, or sons for lost relatives. Many of those thus brought in had been born among the Indians or had lived with them for so long as to forget their own people. These clung piteously to their savage friends, begging that they might not be separated from them, and a number of these afterward effected an escape from the soldiers, in order to return to their beloved forest homes.

As group after group came in, Edith Hester scanned them eagerly in search of a familiar face. At length she saw it, and her eyes lighted with pleasure as she and Christie again met. He was escorted by two venerable warriors, one of whom was the father of the woman whose white husband had slain her for her scalp. While Edith and Christie were eagerly talking, this Indian standing quietly near them suddenly uttered an exclamation of rage, raised his rifle and fired at a white man who was passing. It was the miscreant, David Owens; and as he fell dead the whole camp was instantly in an uproar. The unresisting avenger would have been killed on the spot but for the determined protection of Edith and Christie. As it was, he was placed under arrest and held for trial on the following day.

At this trial, after Christie's testimony and that of several Indians had been taken, Edith Hester delivered such a passionate and convincing plea in behalf of the venerable warrior who had thus avenged the foul murder of his daughter and grandchildren that, to the gratification of the entire assembly, Bouquet ordered him to be acquitted and set free.

With the happy ending of this trial, while Edith was surrounded by a group of officers and receiving their congratulations, a young Indian forced his way through the circle, gave one searching look at the girl's face, and with an almost inarticulate cry of "Edith!" threw his arms about her in a joyful embrace. The scandalized officers were about to lay violent hands on the young savage, when to their amazement, they saw that her arms were about his neck, and that with her fair head on his shoulder she was sobbing hysterically.

In another moment Christie had seized one of his hands and was proclaiming the astounding news that the young Indian was none other than Donald Hester, ensign in His Majesty's regiment of Royal Americans, and long since reported dead.

For nearly half an hour the excited group exchanged an uninterrupted stream of questions and congratulations, mingled with laughter and tears. Then it began to move slowly in the direction of headquarters.

All this time there had been standing a short distance away an Indian youth, and an Indian maiden whose beauty attracted much attention and many outspoken remarks from the soldiers who sauntered past with rude stares and ruder laughter. The girl flushed, glanced about her indignantly, and finally as Edith and Donald began to move away, said in a low tone to her companion:--

"Let us go. They have no thought for us. We are no longer wanted."

So they disappeared; and when, a little later, Donald came back in eager search for Ah-mo and Atoka, they were nowhere to be found nor could he gain any information concerning them.

CHAPTER XL
THE PRINCESS ANSWERS DONALD'S QUESTION

While the army of Bouquet was operating in the south and reducing to submission the tribes of the Ohio valley, another force under command of Colonel Bradstreet, skirted the southern shore of Lake Erie, destroying Indian villages wherever they were found and finally reached Fort Detroit. Thus was the long siege of that frontier post raised, and after fifteen months of close confinement within its palisades the weary garrison were once more free to venture forth, without the risk of being ambushed by an ever vigilant foe. Treaties were signed with all the chiefs of that region, save only Pontiac, who, filled with bitter grief at the failure of the great project to which he had devoted the energies of his life, sullenly retired to his forest stronghold on the Maumee. From there he gave out, that if by spring he had not raised a sufficient force to renew his struggle against the hated redcoats, then would he visit Sir William Johnson, whom alone he recognized as representing the English king, and sign a treaty.

So it happened that the great chief, accompanied by such a retinue as became his rank, presented himself before the walls of Fort Oswego early in the following June and was saluted by a salvo of artillery. Sir William had journeyed that far to meet him, and here the treaty was signed by which Pontiac bound himself to fight no more against the English. After the formalities were concluded, the Ottawa chieftain remained in that vicinity for several weeks as the guest of the governor.

About this time the Bullens reached New York from a flying trip to Oswego, where the paymaster had been summoned on business. Madam Bullen, whom we have long known as Madam Rothsay, always accompanied her husband on such journeys. She declared that both he and "Tummas," who had long since been reluctantly surrendered by the Indians, were so incapable of caring for themselves in the wilderness, that her presence was absolutely necessary to protect them from its dangers.

To this the little paymaster answered that the wilderness had no dangers save such as could be overcome by a man of brains and ingenuity, but that he was always glad to have Madam Bullen accompany him on his trips, and thereby escape, for a while, the perilous cares and anxieties of city life.

From this Oswego trip, which had to do with providing a great quantity of presents for Pontiac and his followers, they returned to their spacious town house on the Bowling Green in time to give a grand ball on the eve of Edith Hester's wedding to Lieutenant James Christie.

Donald was in town, of course, and would appear in uniform for the last time at this ball, as he had resigned from the army in order to devote his whole attention to the great estate left by his father.

"When I rebuild Tawtry House, I shall want you and Edith to come and live with me," he said to Christie, "for without you the loneliness will be horrible."

"I'm afraid you'll have to bear it, old man, for I'm not inclined to give up soldiering yet awhile, and especially so soon after promotion," replied the lieutenant, with a laugh. "But you can easily banish loneliness by installing a mistress in Tawtry House. I'm sure there are plenty of pretty girls in New York who would fill the position charmingly."

"Perhaps there are," answered Donald, indifferently. "I must confess, though, that I have yet to meet one of them whom I could fancy presiding gracefully over the hospitalities of a forest castle."

In truth Donald had not enjoyed his season of New York life, and was ever drawing unfavorable comparisons between it and his previous winter spent so happily in a wilderness hut, amid the mighty forests of the distant Wisconsin. He rarely alluded to those days now, but in his heart of hearts he fondly cherished their memories.

Had the ball given by the Bullens been in honor of any person save his own dear sister, Donald would have excused himself from attendance, so weary was he of such festivities. As it was, he dropped in very late, when the dancing was at its height, and stood for a while listlessly watching the gay scene from one of the entrances to the ball-room. Suddenly he started and leaned eagerly forward. A girl with the bearing of a princess had just swept past him, leaning on the arm of General Gage, commander-in-chief of His Majesty's forces in America. She was robed in corn-colored silk and wore a string of great pearls twined in the jetty braids of her hair. As her dress brushed Donald, he seemed to feel the breath of the forest on his cheek.

"Who is she?" he asked of a young officer standing beside him.

"Who? Oh! The girl the general is so taken with? The belle of the evening? The sensation of the hour? Surely you don't need to be told who she is?"

"But I do," replied Donald, impatiently; "for I have only just come."

"Ah! Well then, she is--To tell you the truth, I don't know exactly who she is, except that she is an Indian princess from the far west, and some say that she is the daughter of Pontiac himself. But she was educated in France, and all that sort of thing, you know. They say she is worth--" Here the speaker paused, for his listener had departed.

Shortly afterwards, Donald Hester was the most envied man in the room; for the beauty of the ball was leaning on his arm, smiling up in his face and talking to him with all the familiarity of old acquaintanceship.

"Lucky dog, that Hester!" remarked one dapper youth to another.

"Yes. They say she once saved him from the stake or something of the kind, and that he has her monogram tattooed on his arm, don't you know? Romantic, awfully."

Out on a broad veranda, from which they could see a flood of moon silver flecking the waters of the bay, Donald was asking Ah-mo many questions. How did she happen to be there? Where had she come from? Why had he not known of her arrival sooner? Did she know that Edith was to be married? Why had she left them so mysteriously and unkindly on the Muskingum the year before?

To these the girl made answer that she had come from Oswego with her kind friend, Madam Bullen, to be bridesmaid at the wedding of her dear friend, Edith Hester.

"So that is Edith's mystery!" cried Donald, who had tried in vain to find out who was to act in that capacity on the morrow.

"Possibly," assented Ah-mo, with the dear rippling laugh that had haunted the young ensign ever since he first heard it on the far-away Detroit. "And now, Mr. Hester, that--"

" Hester? It was not Hester on the banks of the Wisconsin, Ah-mo."

"But that was a year and more ago. Besides, you were not in uniform, then. Do you know I don't think I like you in a red coat, half so well as in buckskin?"

"If it were possible I would discard it this moment," cried Donald, "and I promise you, that after this night, I will never wear it again. But, speaking of dress, Ah-mo, while you are beautiful beyond description in this silken robe, I can't but think that you were still more so in the fawn skin and fur dress that Atoka and I helped you make in Beaver Castle."

So they talked of what had been and what was to be, and of Donald's plans for Tawtry House, until suddenly he said:--

"And now, Ah-mo, I want to ask you the most important question of all. Will you--I mean, can you--"

"Come in to supper," interrupted Paymaster Bullen, bustling out on the veranda at that moment. "Who is it? You, Donald, and you, Ah-mo, my dear girl? Why, there won't be a bite left, if you don't hurry. Never saw such feeders in my life. 'Pon honor, I never did."

"And I didn't have a chance to ask my question," whispered Donald, disconsolately.

"Perhaps you will have a better chance the next time we meet," replied Ah-mo, mischievously.

On the following day came the wedding, with the genuine sensation of an Indian princess as bridesmaid, and opinion was evenly divided as to which was the loveliest,--she, or the bride herself.

On the day after, when Donald called at the Bullens', with his question trembling on his lips, he was astounded and bewildered to learn that Ah-mo had left the evening before on a swift-sailing sloop for Albany. From there she would hasten to Oswego and rejoin her father, who only awaited her coming to start for his distant western home.

"But, sir," said "Tummas," who in all the glory of a gorgeous new livery, had just opened the door, "the young lady left a note for you, hand 'ere it is."

Hastily tearing open the dainty billet thus handed him, Donald read:--

"If your question concerns the belle of a New York ball-room, it had best remain unasked. If it is intended for a simple Indian girl, it had best be asked among the lodges of her people."

A month later the question was asked, and answered very much to Donald's satisfaction; while he, clad in buckskin, and Ah-mo dressed as were the other girls of her tribe, drifted in a canoe on the placid surface of the Detroit river. They were married in the quaint little chapel of the fort, and, as Pontiac gave his beautiful daughter into the arms of him, who was now become doubly his son, he said:--

"May the Great Spirit, the All-seeing Eye of the Magic Circle, who looks alike upon his red children of the forest, and his white children from beyond the salt waters, forever bless this union of the Totem of the Beaver with the Totem of the Bear."

THE END.

www.bookjungle.com *email: sales@bookjungle.com fax: 630-214-0564 mail: Book Jungle PO Box 2226 Champaign, IL 61825*

The Codes Of Hammurabi And Moses
W. W. Davies

QTY

The discovery of the Hammurabi Code is one of the greatest achievements of archaeology, and is of paramount interest, not only to the student of the Bible, but also to all those interested in ancient history...

Religion   **ISBN:** *1-59462-338-4*   Pages:132
MSRP $12.95

The Theory of Moral Sentiments
Adam Smith

QTY

This work from 1749. contains original theories of con- science amd moral judgment and it is the foundation for systemof morals.

Philosophy   **ISBN:** *1-59462-777-0*   Pages:536
MSRP $19.95

Jessica's First Prayer
Hesba Stretton

QTY

In a screened and secluded corner of one of the many railway-bridges which span the streets of London there could be seen a few years ago, from five o'clock every morning until half past eight, a tidily set-out coffee-stall, consisting of a trestle and board, upon which stood two large tin cans, with a small fire of charcoal burning under each so as to keep the coffee boiling during the early hours of the morning when the work-people were thronging into the city on their way to their daily toil...

Childrens   **ISBN:** *1-59462-373-2*   Pages:84
MSRP $9.95

My Life and Work
Henry Ford

QTY

Henry Ford revolutionized the world with his implementation of mass production for the Model T automobile. Gain valuable business insight into his life and work with his own auto-biography... "We have only started on our development of our country we have not as yet, with all our talk of wonderful progress, done more than scratch the surface. The progress has been wonderful enough but..."

Biographies/   **ISBN:** *1-59462-198-5*   Pages:300
MSRP $21.95

www.bookjungle.com *email: sales@bookjungle.com fax: 630-214-0564 mail: Book Jungle PO Box 2226 Champaign, IL 61825*

The Art of Cross-Examination
Francis Wellman

QTY

I presume it is the experience of every author, after his first book is published upon an important subject, to be almost overwhelmed with a wealth of ideas and illustrations which could readily have been included in his book, and which to his own mind, at least, seem to make a second edition inevitable. Such certainly was the case with me; and when the first edition had reached its sixth impression in five months, I rejoiced to learn that it seemed to my publishers that the book had met with a sufficiently favorable reception to justify a second and considerably enlarged edition. ...

Reference   ISBN: *1-59462-647-2*

Pages:412
MSRP *$19.95*

On the Duty of Civil Disobedience
Henry David Thoreau

QTY

Thoreau wrote his famous essay, On the Duty of Civil Disobedience, as a protest against an unjust but popular war and the immoral but popular institution of slave-owning. He did more than write—he declined to pay his taxes, and was hauled off to gaol in consequence. Who can say how much this refusal of his hastened the end of the war and of slavery ?

Law   ISBN: *1-59462-747-9*

Pages:48
MSRP *$7.45*

Dream Psychology Psychoanalysis for Beginners
Sigmund Freud

QTY

Sigmund Freud, born Sigismund Schlomo Freud (May 6, 1856 - September 23, 1939), was a Jewish-Austrian neurologist and psychiatrist who co-founded the psychoanalytic school of psychology. Freud is best known for his theories of the unconscious mind, especially involving the mechanism of repression; his redefinition of sexual desire as mobile and directed towards a wide variety of objects; and his therapeutic techniques, especially his understanding of transference in the therapeutic relationship and the presumed value of dreams as sources of insight into unconscious desires.

Psychology   ISBN: *1-59462-905-6*

Pages:196
MSRP *$15.45*

The Miracle of Right Thought
Orison Swett Marden

QTY

Believe with all of your heart that you will do what you were made to do. When the mind has once formed the habit of holding cheerful, happy, prosperous pictures, it will not be easy to form the opposite habit. It does not matter how improbable or how far away this realization may see, or how dark the prospects may be, if we visualize them as best we can, as vividly as possible, hold tenaciously to them and vigorously struggle to attain them, they will gradually become actualized, realized in the life. But a desire, a longing without endeavor, a yearning abandoned or held indifferently will vanish without realization.

Self Help   ISBN: *1-59462-644-8*

Pages:360
MSRP *$25.45*

www.bookjungle.com *email: sales@bookjungle.com fax: 630-214-0564 mail: Book Jungle PO Box 2226 Champaign, IL 61825*

QTY

| | **The Rosicrucian Cosmo-Conception Mystic Christianity** *by* **Max Heindel** | **ISBN: 1-59462-188-8** | **$38.95** |

The Rosicrucian Cosmo-conception is not dogmatic, neither does it appeal to any other authority than the reason of the student. It is: not controversial, but is: sent forth in the, hope that it may help to clear... — *New Age/Religion Pages 646*

Abandonment To Divine Providence *by* **Jean-Pierre de Caussade**   **ISBN: 1-59462-228-0**   **$25.95**
"The Rev. Jean Pierre de Caussade was one of the most remarkable spiritual writers of the Society of Jesus in France in the 18th Century. His death took place at Toulouse in 1751. His works have gone through many editions and have been republished... — *Inspirational/Religion Pages 400*

Mental Chemistry *by* **Charles Haanel**   **ISBN: 1-59462-192-6**   **$23.95**
Mental Chemistry allows the change of material conditions by combining and appropriately utilizing the power of the mind. Much like applied chemistry creates something new and unique out of careful combinations of chemicals the mastery of mental chemistry... — *New Age Pages 354*

The Letters of Robert Browning and Elizabeth Barret Barrett 1845-1846 vol II   **ISBN: 1-59462-193-4**   **$35.95**
by **Robert Browning** *and* **Elizabeth Barrett**   *Biographies Pages 596*

Gleanings In Genesis (volume I) *by* **Arthur W. Pink**   **ISBN: 1-59462-130-6**   **$27.45**
Appropriately has Genesis been termed "the seed plot of the Bible" for in it we have, in germ form, almost all of the great doctrines which are afterwards fully developed in the books of Scripture which follow... — *Religion/Inspirational Pages 420*

The Master Key *by* **L. W. de Laurence**   **ISBN: 1-59462-001-6**   **$30.95**
In no branch of human knowledge has there been a more lively increase of the spirit of research during the past few years than in the study of Psychology, Concentration and Mental Discipline. The requests for authentic lessons in Thought Control, Mental Discipline and... — *New Age/Business Pages 422*

The Lesser Key Of Solomon Goetia *by* **L. W. de Laurence**   **ISBN: 1-59462-092-X**   **$9.95**
This translation of the first book of the "Lemegton" which is now for the first time made accessible to students of Talismanic Magic was done, after careful collation and edition, from numerous Ancient Manuscripts in Hebrew, Latin, and French... — *New Age/Occult Pages 92*

Rubaiyat Of Omar Khayyam *by* **Edward Fitzgerald**   **ISBN:** *1-59462-332-5*   **$13.95**
Edward Fitzgerald, whom the world has already learned, in spite of his own efforts to remain within the shadow of anonymity, to look upon as one of the rarest poets of the century, was born at Bredfield, in Suffolk, on the 31st of March, 1809. He was the third son of John Purcell... — *Music Pages 172*

Ancient Law *by* **Henry Maine**   **ISBN: 1-59462-128-4**   **$29.95**
The chief object of the following pages is to indicate some of the earliest ideas of mankind, as they are reflected in Ancient Law, and to point out the relation of those ideas to modern thought. — *Religiom/History Pages 452*

Far-Away Stories *by* **William J. Locke**   **ISBN: 1-59462-129-2**   **$19.45**
"Good wine needs no bush, but a collection of mixed vintages does. And this book is just such a collection. Some of the stories I do not want to remain buried for ever in the museum files of dead magazine-numbers an author's not unpardonable vanity..." — *Fiction Pages 272*

Life of David Crockett *by* **David Crockett**   **ISBN: 1-59462-250-7**   **$27.45**
"Colonel David Crockett was one of the most remarkable men of the times in which he lived. Born in humble life, but gifted with a strong will, an indomitable courage, and unremitting perseverance... — *Biographies/New Age Pages 424*

Lip-Reading *by* **Edward Nitchie**   **ISBN: 1-59462-206-X**   **$25.95**
Edward B. Nitchie, founder of the New York School for the Hard of Hearing, now the Nitchie School of Lip-Reading, Inc, wrote "LIP-READING Principles and Practice". The development and perfecting of this meritorious work on lip-reading was an undertaking... — *How-to Pages 400*

A Handbook of Suggestive Therapeutics, Applied Hypnotism, Psychic Science   **ISBN: 1-59462-214-0**   **$24.95**
by **Henry Munro**   *Health/New Age/Health/Self-help Pages 376*

A Doll's House: and Two Other Plays *by* **Henrik Ibsen**   **ISBN: 1-59462-112-8**   **$19.95**
Henrik Ibsen created this classic when in revolutionary 1848 Rome. Introducing some striking concepts in playwriting for the realist genre, this play has been studied the world over. — *Fiction/Classics/Plays 308*

The Light of Asia *by* **sir Edwin Arnold**   **ISBN: 1-59462-204-3**   **$13.95**
In this poetic masterpiece, Edwin Arnold describes the life and teachings of Buddha. The man who was to become known as Buddha to the world was born as Prince Gautama of India but he rejected the worldly riches and abandoned the reigns of power when... — *Religion/History/Biographies Pages 170*

The Complete Works of Guy de Maupassant *by* **Guy de Maupassant**   **ISBN: 1-59462-157-8**   **$16.95**
"For days and days, nights and nights, I had dreamed of that first kiss which was to consecrate our engagement, and I knew not on what spot I should put my lips..." — *Fiction/Classics Pages 240*

The Art of Cross-Examination *by* **Francis L. Wellman**   **ISBN: 1-59462-309-0**   **$26.95**
Written by a renowned trial lawyer, Wellman imparts his experience and uses case studies to explain how to use psychology to extract desired information through questioning. — *How-to/Science/Reference Pages 408*

Answered or Unanswered? *by* **Louisa Vaughan**   **ISBN: 1-59462-248-5**   **$10.95**
Miracles of Faith in China   *Religion Pages 112*

The Edinburgh Lectures on Mental Science (1909) *by* **Thomas**   **ISBN: 1-59462-008-3**   **$11.95**
This book contains the substance of a course of lectures recently given by the writer in the Queen Street Hall, Edinburgh. Its purpose is to indicate the Natural Principles governing the relation between Mental Action and Material Conditions... — *New Age/Psychology Pages 148*

Ayesha *by* **H. Rider Haggard**   **ISBN: 1-59462-301-5**   **$24.95**
Verily and indeed it is the unexpected that happens! Probably if there was one person upon the earth from whom the Editor of this, and of a certain previous history, did not expect to hear again... — *Classics Pages 380*

Ayala's Angel *by* **Anthony Trollope**   **ISBN: 1-59462-352-X**   **$29.95**
The two girls were both pretty, but Lucy who was twenty-one who supposed to be simple and comparatively unattractive, whereas Ayala was credited, as her Bombwhat romantic name might show, with poetic charm and a taste for romance. Ayala when her father died was nineteen... — *Fiction Pages 484*

The American Commonwealth *by* **James Bryce**   **ISBN: 1-59462-286-8**   **$34.45**
An interpretation of American democratic political theory. It examines political mechanics and society from the perspective of Scotsman James Bryce — *Politics Pages 572*

Stories of the Pilgrims *by* **Margaret P. Pumphrey**   **ISBN: 1-59462-116-0**   **$17.95**
This book explores pilgrims religious oppression in England as well as their escape to Holland and eventual crossing to America on the Mayflower, and their early days in New England... — *History Pages 268*

www.bookjungle.com *email:* sales@bookjungle.com *fax:* 630-214-0564 *mail:* Book Jungle PO Box 2226 Champaign, IL 61825

			QTY
The Fasting Cure *by Sinclair Upton*	ISBN: *1-59462-222-1*	**$13.95**	
In the Cosmopolitan Magazine for May, 1910, and in the Contemporary Review (London) for April, 1910, I published an article dealing with my experiences in fasting. I have written a great many magazine articles, but never one which attracted so much attention...	New Age/Self Help/Health	Pages 164	
Hebrew Astrology *by Sepharial*	ISBN: *1-59462-308-2*	**$13.45**	
In these days of advanced thinking it is a matter of common observation that we have left many of the old landmarks behind and that we are now pressing forward to greater heights and to a wider horizon than that which represented the mind-content of our progenitors...	Astrology	Pages 144	
Thought Vibration or The Law of Attraction in the Thought World	ISBN: *1-59462-127-6*	**$12.95**	
by William Walker Atkinson	Psychology/Religion	Pages 144	
Optimism *by Helen Keller*	ISBN: *1-59462-108-X*	**$15.95**	
Helen Keller was blind, deaf, and mute since 19 months old, yet famously learned how to overcome these handicaps, communicate with the world, and spread her lectures promoting optimism. An inspiring read for everyone...	Biographies/Inspirational	Pages 84	
Sara Crewe *by Frances Burnett*	ISBN: *1-59462-360-0*	**$9.45**	
In the first place, Miss Minchin lived in London. Her home was a large, dull, tall one, in a large, dull square, where all the houses were alike, and all the sparrows were alike, and where all the door-knockers made the same heavy sound...	Childrens/Classic	Pages 88	
The Autobiography of Benjamin Franklin *by Benjamin Franklin*	ISBN: *1-59462-135-7*	**$24.95**	
The Autobiography of Benjamin Franklin has probably been more extensively read than any other American historical work, and no other book of its kind has had such ups and downs of fortune. Franklin lived for many years in England, where he was agent...	Biographies/History	Pages 332	

Name

Email

Telephone

Address

City, State ZIP

☐ Credit Card   ☐ Check / Money Order

Credit Card Number

Expiration Date

Signature

Please Mail to: Book Jungle
                    PO Box 2226
                    Champaign, IL 61825
or Fax to: 630-214-0564

ORDERING INFORMATION

web: *www.bookjungle.com*
email: *sales@bookjungle.com*
fax: *630-214-0564*
mail: *Book Jungle PO Box 2226 Champaign, IL 61825*
or PayPal *to sales@bookjungle.com*

Please contact us for bulk discounts

DIRECT-ORDER TERMS

20% Discount if You Order Two or More Books
Free Domestic Shipping!
Accepted: Master Card, Visa, Discover, American Express

www.ingramcontent.com/pod-product-compliance
Lightning Source LLC
Chambersburg PA
CBHW081231170426
43198CB00017B/2722